Powerful
People
Have
Powerful
Relationships

A  Book

Powerful People Have Powerful Relationships

Your Daily Guide to Creating People Connections

Peter Biadasz and Marilyn S. Possett, L.C.S.W.

A  Book

iUniverse, Inc.

New York Lincoln Shanghai

Powerful People Have Powerful Relationships
Your Daily Guide to Creating People Connections

iUniverse books may be ordered through booksellers or by contacting:

iUniverse
2021 Pine Lake Road, Suite 100
Lincoln, NE 68512
www.iuniverse.com
1-800-Authors (1-800-288-4677)

The information, ideas, and suggestions in this book are not intended as a substitute for professional advice. Before following any suggestions contained in this book, consult a professional. Neither the author nor the publisher shall be liable or responsible for any loss or damage allegedly arising as a consequence of your use or application of any information or suggestions in this book.

ISBN-13: 978-0-595-41138-2 (pbk)
ISBN-13: 978-0-595-85496-7 (ebk)
ISBN-10: 0-595-41138-X (pbk)
ISBN-10: 0-595-85496-6 (ebk)

Printed in the United States of America

Foreword

By
Ramona S. Moody, L.C.S.W.
Psychotherapist ~ Outpatient Services
Laureate Psychiatric Clinic and Hospital

When talking with my professional colleagues, we all seem to agree that the one key characteristic of a powerful person is their ability to create and maintain good interpersonal relationships. From practical experience we know without a doubt that most people desire power. But, what does the term really mean? That is, being powerful, having power, and being a power-driven person.

For me, a power-person is one who has considerable control over their own destiny in life. You see, power and control can be synonymous. When one is powerful they are strong and influential. They are not physically nasty and tough, but they are energetic, healthy, resolute, intelligent, pleasant, effective, proficient, reliable, persuasive, passionate, courageous, and successful.

Individuals who are truly powerful wield great power over themselves. They may have much authority and command over others, but power-people understand that their personal clout is really based upon their influence with people and not the mere right to rule. Their true power comes from their ability to affect others in a positive and productive manner. It is manifested by their great ability to do, to act with force and charismatic sway. It doesn't come from dominion and overpowering control.

To have or garner the masterful might of personal power, we need strong and positive relationships in all facets of our lives. We need powerful connections with other human beings to be successful. We need exciting and hardy associations whether they are in a marriage, familial relationship, parent/child bond, friendship, or employee and employer association.

For the majority of us, creating and sustaining sound relationships is not a given, an endowment. Developing solid associations with other individuals is a learned behavior. When we were growing up we may or may not have been instructed well in effective relationships. In our personal development, we may or may not even know that we have weak interpersonal skills. We may have blind spots, bad habits, and uncultivated behavior patterns when it comes to interacting with others. These weaknesses may be contributing to our difficulty in dealing with people. They can be encumbering our reach for success. They can be inhibiting our talents. They can be retarding our ability to become a power-person.

My close colleague and friend, Marilyn Possett, and her co-author, Peter Biadasz, have written this book to help people develop and sustain fun and functional relationships. The manuscript is designed like a workbook. It is a one year journey into discovering what makes and takes for good relationships. It is written with thought provoking quotes from powerful people about interacting with others. Each day, for six months, there is a simple and straightforward exercise that you complete. The book is laid out so that after a half year you can reevaluate all of your work. In this way you reinforce the practices prescribed in the book. The authors approach is a fast and easy method to daily changes that cascade into behaviors that can be positive and permanent. It is like rain drops making a river. These are habits and behavior patterns that help people with strong relationships overflow with power.

relationship

NOUN:

1. The condition or fact of being related; connection or association.

2. Connection by blood or marriage; kinship.

3. A particular type of connection existing between people related to or having dealings with each other:
has a close relationship with his siblings.

4. A romantic or sexual involvement.

American Heritage®Dictionary

Dedications

This book is dedicated to my husband, Richard, who has always encouraged me to be more than I was. Together we have formed a wonderful lifetime relationship.

—Marilyn S. Possett, L.C.S.W.

This book is dedicated to my son Andy and daughter Danielle. It is through them that I have learned lessons in relationships that go beyond words and experienced a love that transcends depth beyond comprehension.

—Peter Biadasz

Acknowledgements

Thank you to my family, friends, colleagues, and clients who have taught me so much about relationships. A special thanks to my great friend, Ramona S. Moody, L.C.S.W., who has been with me throughout my career, and with whom I can always share my thoughts and ideas.

—Marilyn S. Possett, L.C.S.W.

Thank you to my family, my friends and business associates; you add so much to my personal and professional life. Even though I may not always show it, know that my appreciation runs very deep.

—Peter Biadasz

Why Read This Book?

Every time we come into contact with another person a relationship is formed. It may be casual or permanent, loose or tight, shallow or deep, personal or professional. As you can see, relationships can range from the incidental we may have with the clerk at the dry cleaners to the intimate one we have with our spouse. Everyone has associations with other people in their daily lives. Thus, the better we are at creating and maintaining them, the happier, more peaceful, and meaningful life will be for ourselves. POWERFUL PEOPLE HAVE POWERFUL RELATIONSHIPS: *Your Daily Guide to Creating People Connections* is the book for you if you want to add the strength and energy of these elements to your associations with family, friends and fellow travelers.

Having power in a relationship may denote, to some, holding control or domination over another person. In the context of this book power is used to mean the vim, vigor, vitality, and virtue in your personal involvement with others. Said differently, it is the soundness, strength, and stalwartness of your continued attachment with people. Therefore, to create and maintain powerful relationships means to have your associations with your fellow man be meaningful, pleasant, and satisfying.

Power is that essential energy, intensity, and well-being that you contribute to a relationship. It is what makes the association truly valuable, full of meaning, and gives it longevity. One's positive power from relationships produces an agreeable effect upon the mind, body, and spirit. It makes our attachments merry, pleasing, relaxed, and fun. It is a healthy fulfillment that is rewarding and free from doubt and anxiety. These are the reasons why powerful people have powerful relationships.

Relationships are difficult to develop and sustain. This is so because the interpersonal skills needed to manifest and maintain satisfactory relationships are generally not taught while growing up. This ability is a learned behavior through observation and, most often, by trial and error. Throughout life we develop habits in relating to others. Sometimes we develop good practices that are useful, such as good listening skills; and at other times we develop unpleasant behavior, such as having to always be right. But new relationship skills can be learned and hurtful patterns changed. Behavior changes slowly, however, with day-by-day reminders to yourself, as well as practice and application; and those new-found capabilities can be imbedded into your everyday culture.

Right now you are reading a one-of-a-kind book. There is nothing else like it on the bookshelf. The text is unique because of its multidimensional nature. The manuscript focuses primarily on relationships between spouses, family members, and friends. But the lessons can also be applied to business and casual associations. The book is a practical, inspirational, and educational guide on developing the skills needed to form more pleasant and productive relationships. Although the book is comprehensively compelling, it is still simple and easy. It's simple to read and the assignments are easy to complete. This format allows you to learn new relationship proficiency each and every day and encourages you to practice and apply your new found knowledge. It gives you a fresh awareness of the way you relate to others and suggestions for positive change. For you see, this book is a once a day, fast and easy, excursion into having more dynamic relationships and therefore, being a more powerful person.

This book is not intended to solve all of your relationship issues. Many factors come into play in building relationships and this book does not address all of them. If you are struggling with a serious problem, we urge you to seek professional help. We realize that there are always other people involved in relationships who have their own unique ways of relating. The intention of this book is to help you become aware, in a general sense, of the way you are currently relating to others and to become mindful that there may be other ways to conduct yourself.

Read this book; do the exercises every day and apply what you are learning to your relationships. By the time you are finished, you should be a more knowledgeable person with new confidence in your personal and professional relationships. As you progress through this book, you will discover both your good relationship patterns and your poor ones. You will grow more confident each day by building on your strengths and reducing your limitations.

Each day you will learn an inspirational quote. The quotes were chosen for their content and message rather than the origin of the quote. Be that as it may, fact-find the authors. In doing so you may just become a more well-rounded individual. It can be highly interesting to learn about the quote source and why, when, and where the author may have expressed them. With your research and education about powerful people you emerge a renaissance person. Being able to discuss what you have learned will help you to be a more conversant, interesting, and sought after person. This ability may help you feel more at ease in associations with others. It will make you more powerful.

By completing the daily lessons, you become increasingly knowledgeable and educated about relationships. Give thoughtful consideration to the lessons and what you gain by doing them thoroughly. Simply finishing the tasks, however, will not yield a successful relationship unless you actually apply what you have learned. Just making a list or writing your thoughts down will not be of assistance unless you integrate the example into your everyday behavior. It is one thing to know what to do and yet another to truly do it. Work on it and make it work in your relationships. If you are diligent in your work, it works.

A unique bonus in the book is that you can reflect upon your efforts after six months. This process gives you an honest chance to fully reevaluate your relationships and discover if what you are doing is working for you. By learning the daily lessons and applying one skill each day into your business and personal world you will become more learned and confident with your relationship skills. And as you sow, you will reap wonderful individual benefits. Become a power-person by creating and maintaining powerful relationships.

Note: You may want to consider utilizing two copies of this book, one for your personal relationships and another for your professional associations. Each type of relationship has within itself a unique dynamic, and thus, may be approached differently. Keep one copy of this book in your home and another copy at the office. In this way, you have the opportunity to become more proficient in the connections of life; commercial and private.

Table of Contents

Preface

RELATONSHIPS...*the connection between two or more people or groups and their involvement with each other, especially as regard to how they behave and feel toward each other and communicate or cooperate* (Encarta Dictionary: English). Connections are all around us: spouse, children, siblings, partners, friends, fellow workers, neighbors, and ourselves. They are ubiquitous, sometimes demanding, and changing everyday. This book was born out of the desire for people to have better, healthier, and more satisfying relationships in all facets of their lives.

Interacting with people can be at times both enjoyable and bothersome. Good interpersonal associations need to be ever-present and ever-lasing. The unfortunate fact is that people often do not acquire the necessary life-skills to interact well with their fellow travelers. Learning to build and maintain healthy relationships is an important part of life that we are confronted with everyday. It seems that there are two ways we develop relationships. We can go into a relationship with a laid foundation on which to build; or we can learn through trial and error from the ground up. Most times the approach is somewhere in the middle which produces a little hit and a lot of miss. The purpose of this book is to improve your aim so that you can not only hit the target more often, but strike the bulls-eye in relationships.

Our book takes one year to complete. It is an interesting and easy read. We have stimulating quotations and thoughtful exercises. The book's simplicity is its compelling characteristic. We understand that people are busy in today's fast-paced world. Finding time to do everything that needs to be done can be a challenge. Our approach is to encourage you to spend a little time each day on a subject matter. Everyday, for one-half year, you pause for a few minutes and reflect upon your human associations; your connections; your relationships. Then, you complete a single exercise and imbed that knowledge into your real life. This practice creates consciousness and this awareness stimulates transition; a change for the better. In the second six months, you review and critique the previously finished assignments and exercises. This repetition reinforces a new learned behavior. If needed, after the reevaluation, you make any necessary further modifications. From this simple process you develop small individual daily good habits that cascade into new ways of living; into new understandings about yourself; into new positive patterns of interacting with people; into you becoming a more powerful person.

The *quotations* and *assignments* in this book will not only challenge you to examine and improve upon your existing relationships, but will also encourage you to expand on all of your potential associations. Please know that change can come slowly, but surely. In our modern culture, time is at a premium. We fully understand the challenge of change. We have a high regard for your time and resources. This is why we have written this book to span an entire year. Our approach gives you the time and method to change into a powerful person. This book will impact every area of your being. Daily, as you read and fill in the blanks for your life, know that you are becoming more proficient in your relationships. Understand that your new found knowledge brings confidence into your human connections. Enjoy the journey that you are undertaking. There are many rewards, and maybe even a few surprises. We pray that you experience incredible success in all of your relationships.

Peter Biadasz and Marilyn S. Posset, L.C.S.W.

ॐ ॐ

(Before proceeding, turn to page 189 to read more about the authors and gain a better frame of reference and perspective regarding them and this book.)

A Note from the Authors

The manner in which we connect with others can impact all aspects of our lives. During my practice as an individual and marital therapist I have met many people with varying problems. They may be having physical difficulties, such as headaches, stomach distress, or muscle tension or they may complain of anxiety, depressed mood, or inability to concentrate. But no matter what the presenting problem might be it very often relates back to a relationship difficulty.

The manner of associations we have in our lives can affect physical and mental health in a variety of ways. Family problems cause distress, intimate difficulties cause heartache, and occupational dilemmas cause tension. When someone complains of nervousness, sleeplessness, appetite loss, or excess frustration and irritability, we examine these issues and very often find that what lies at the foundation of the suffering is a struggle with some personal connection. Sometimes people are too focused on others and are over-caretakers, doing much more for others than is needed. Other times folks are focused too much on themselves and need to look at how that behavior is affecting their lives.

Discovering how to develop, manage, and maintain healthy connections can clear up a variety of obstacles in life. Honing your people and interpersonal skills may go a long way in life improvement.

Use this book as a primer to examine the way you relate to people. Practice the parts where you think you need improvement and reinforce the sections in which you are doing well. See if paying attention to your relationship skills helps in all facets of your life. Remember: It's all about relationships!

Happy life building!!

Marilyn S. Possett, L.C.S.W.

This book is simplistic yet complicated, just like real life relationships. I want to make you aware of a challenge you will face greater and greater as you dive into this book. However be aware that even if approached properly, the challenge will be addressed, but may never be resolved.

While some challenges in relationships can be traced to differences in personality, upbringing, social differences, etc., I am specifically referring to the differences in which the two genders address relationships. It will amaze you, if you are working through this book with a significant other of the opposite sex, how you will see and interpret the same page in totally different ways. As a point of reference, which types of magazines usually address relationship topics, women's or men's? Which gender has a better understanding of communication? Which gender listens better? Can you see the debate brewing?

We men tend to think of ourselves as a fairly simple lot with a list of true needs no greater than the number of fingers on our hand. Yet I have heard many women talk about how complicated we are as a gender. Likewise, I have heard many women say that their true relationship needs are quite simple, but a man just can't figure them out. In the mean time, we men are left wondering as to why these "simple" concepts cannot be clearly explained to us. Get the picture?

Be aware of this situation and learn from it. Do not be frustrated as you attempt to resolve it. Enjoy the journey of learning.

Peter Biadasz

Introduction

What Are Relationships?

The American Heritage Dictionary defines a relationship as the condition or fact of being related, connected, or associated. The connection could be by blood, marriage, kinship, or just an association between people having dealings with each other. It could be a romantic or sexual involvement. Every time we have an interaction with someone we form an association, no matter how fleeting. When you purchase groceries you briefly relate to the checkout person, when you make an appointment you interact with the scheduler, and when you marry or have a child you form a lifetime connection.

Unless you are isolated in a cabin in the woods you are experiencing relationships with someone, even if it is only the telemarketer on the telephone. Some relationships are casual, some are formal, some are businesslike, and some are intimate. Some are mixtures and blends. They can be transitory or enduring, joyful or miserable, agreeable or unpleasant, difficult or effortless. Connections with others require give and take, compromise and flexibility, cooperation and patience, tolerance and understanding; and sometimes, persistence and forgiveness.

Good quality associations can help make life more satisfying and fun. Without connections to other people, our lives would be unfulfilled and monotonous. Relationships impact all aspects of our lives.

What (Or Who) Is a Powerful Person?

A powerful person is someone who gets things done when they need to be done. They do it! They do it right! And, they do it right now! Power-driven people are the class President, team captain, chief executive, and community leader. Sometimes they are the nerds of the world. So be careful what you do on the playground. A powerful person always seems to have time for improved performance at work, home, and play. They eat right and exercise. They take time out in their day for reading, whether it is personal or professional. Power people pay attention to themselves and their relationships with other folks. They generally over-see people, but most importantly they manage themselves very well. Powerfully performing individuals control their time, actions, and results. They are self-reliant. Power performers take charge and respon-sibility. They don't play the blame game. They are self-confident, but not cocky. They are highly self-disciplined. They are self-motivated. When called upon to do the job, they get results on time. They do this in both their personal and professional worlds. They always perform powerfully. Power people have created a personal culture, a way of living life, of per-forming at the highest level.

How to Use This Book

This manuscript is styled as an interactive workbook on relationships. It contains simple and straightforward daily exercises. By no means is this book meant to be a comprehensive self-study course on how to interact effectively with people. The purpose of the work is to create a strong individual awareness in the readers about how they relate to others. The intent of the writing is to inform the readers about common sense char-acteristics of connections and associations between individuals and groups. It is not a new theory, but a time-tested practical guide to creat-ing and sustaining powerful relationships. The objective of the exercises is to reinforce these basic principles. The quotations help validate the ele-ments of what make up functional relationships between human beings.

Everyday you are given an opportunity to become more proficient in the skills necessary for powerful relationships. If you complete the daily task as asked, over time you will incrementally amass a compendium of knowledge on people associations. If you then properly apply this learning in your life, the connections with your family, friends, and fellow workers will become more powerful one day at a time.

Six Months Review

This book is a one year journey about relationships. It is divided into two six month segments. The first section has to do with daily quotations and assignments helping to establish a consciousness of our interpersonal skills and behaviors. The exercises help us to identify counterproductive behavior patterns that could be corrected for more successful interactions with the people in our life. The material also identifies new habits that might be established to strengthen the bonds between the people with whom one associates. In the second six months, the reader has the opportunity to add depth, modify and reinforce what was learned during the first part of the program. At the end of one year, you will have addressed the key areas that will make your relationships more powerful.

Sample Illustration

January 1
July 1

"The only way to have a friend is to be one."

Ralph Waldo Emerson

What kind of friend are you? Are you being the type of friend to others that you would like to be your friend? Develop an inventory list of the qualities that make a good friend. Reexamine then, and make certain that you are being one yourself.

Qualities of a good friend:
Dependability, honesty, trustworthiness, fun-loving and non-judgmental.

How I exemplified these qualities with my friends:
Followed through with helping John move on Saturday. Kept the confidence of Mary about her problems at work. Invited Tom to the ballgame on Sunday. Paid his way. Did not criticize when Sue told me she did something in her life of which I did not approve.

Six Months Review:
I continued to practice the above qualities in the interactions with my friends. I followed through every time I made a commitment. I planned fun activities and made sure I presented a relaxed and fun-loving mood. I kept confidences. I need to work on being less judgmental.

About the Quote Sources

If you desire to receive some further rewards from the daily exercises, do research on the people quoted on the pages in this book. You are encouraged to learn about their unique life and special times. Learning how these individuals became power-driven people in their own right can be fascinating, if not educational. If someone happens to be quoted more than once, research the circumstances surrounding the quotation. In the instances of sayings and proverbs, a study into the traditions associated with each aphorism may be instructive. Consider doing the same for the unknown authors. Getting to know the composer of the quote and the particulars surrounding the passages can be a meaningful journey into history. The results of your study and research can be placed in the lines provided which are labeled as "Quotation Source Information." Here we have an important announcement: please understand that in instances in which a quote or manuscript text refers to "him" that the word "her" can simply be substituted.

And please remember…

"The wisdom of the wise, and the experience of the ages, may be preserved by quotation."

~ Benjamin Disraeli

And we say…

Tell me…I'll forget

Show me…I'll remember

Involve me…I'll comprehend

So, get involved to be great, to get better!

HAVE POWERFUL RELATIONSHIPS!

January 1
July 2

"Love forgets mistakes;
nagging about them parts the best of friends."

Solomon

Continuing to bring up someone's mistakes never changes them. Forgiving and accepting someone does more good. Whose mistakes are you nagging about?

Name: _____
_____
_____

How can you forgive and accept?
_____
_____
_____

Six Months Review:
_____
_____
_____

Quotation Source Information:
_____
_____
_____

January 2
July 3

> "We always have choices to make about relationships—all the way from the partners we choose, to the people we associate with and the way we treat them each day."

Marilyn S. Possett, L.C.S.W.

If we keep having the same difficulties in our relationships, the problem may be the people we choose, or it could be the way we choose to treat them. List three people you will interact with today, and detail how you will choose to treat them:

Name: _____
Behavior: _____
_____

Name: _____
Behavior: _____
_____

Name: _____
Behavior: _____
_____

Six Months Review:

_____
_____
_____

Quotation Source Information:

_____
_____
_____

January 3
July 4

"The most important single ingredient in the formula of success is knowing how to get along with people."

Theodore Roosevelt

This is something we usually learn in kindergarten when we learn to share, wait our turn and listen to others. What kind of feedback have you been given about your people skills? Write it here and list any areas that need work:

_____

_____

_____

_____

_____

Six Months Review:

_____

_____

_____

Quotation Source Information:

_____

_____

_____

January 4
July 5

"There is only one person in this world who can ever make you feel discouraged, worried, angry or happy and that person is **you**."

Marilyn S. Possett, L.C.S.W.

This is an entirely new concept for some people. Many of us have learned that we are responsible for making others happy and we forget about our own happiness. You can't really make another person be happy. Each person is responsible for his or her own happiness. This idea could change your life.

List three ways you will make yourself happy today, tomorrow, and next year:

1. _____

_____

2. _____

_____

3. _____

_____

Six Months Review:

_____
_____
_____

Quotation Source Information:

_____
_____
_____

January 5
July 6

"We have not passed that subtle line between childhood and adulthood until we move from the passive voice to the active voice—that is, until we stop saying 'it got lost,' and say 'I lost it.'"

Sydney Harris

One great lesson we want children to learn is to admit they made a mistake. It doesn't have to be such a difficult thing. Admitting responsibility for errors and accepting the consequences is ten times easier than lying about it. What kind of example do you set for others in this area?

List two ways you will take responsibility for your actions today:

1. _____
   _____

2. _____
   _____

Six Months Review:
_____
_____
_____

Quotation Source Information:
_____
_____
_____

January 6
July 7

"The smartest thing I ever said was, 'Help Me!'"

Afflatus

We all need help sometimes and it is not a sign of weak character to ask for help. Think of it this way, if you don't ask someone to help, you rob them of the pleasure one can receive from being of assistance to others.

Today list people you can ask for help and why you would ask that particular person:

Name: _____

Reason: _____

_____

Name: _____

Reason: _____

_____

Name: _____

Reason: _____

_____

Six Months Review:

_____

_____

_____

Quotation Source Information:

_____

_____

_____

January 7
July 8

"Happiness is not the absence of conflict but the ability to cope with it."

Vanpossetski

Often people describe themselves as *conflict avoiders*, and really, most people do not like conflict. However, differences will always be part of life so you had better learn to think about conflict differently. Conflicts are unavoidable challenges that do not determine your happiness but the ability to cope with them may help.

Write down a conflict you are currently having with someone and then list healthy ways to cope with it:

Conflict: _____

Ways to cope:

1. _____
   _____

2. _____
   _____

3. _____
   _____

Six Months Review:

_____
_____
_____

Quotation Source Information:

_____
_____
_____

January 8
July 9

"A good sense of humor is the greatest coping skill."

Marilyn S. Possett, L.C.S.W.

We all know those people who make us laugh with their ability to see humor in most situations. It lightens the moment and seems to pull us back to the present. Are you using your sense of humor in your relationships?

Today list ways you will use your sense of humor to help you maintain a relationship with someone:

1. _____
   _____

2. _____
   _____

3. _____
   _____

4. _____
   _____

Six Months Review:

_____
_____
_____

Quotation Source Information:

_____
_____
_____

January 9
July 10

"True friends are those who,
when you make a fool of yourself,
don't believe that this is a permanent condition."

Erwin Randall

All of us have thought we made a fool of ourselves at one time or another. How did you react when it was in front of one of your friends? Were you embarrassed or were you able to use your sense of humor?

Who are the friends with whom you can relax and be yourself without worrying about how they will think of you?

Names:

_____
_____
_____

Six Months Review:

_____
_____
_____

Quotation Source Information:

_____
_____
_____

January 10
July11

> "The best way to cheer yourself up is
> to try to cheer somebody else up."

Mark Twain

When you are feeling sad or blue that would be a good time to contact someone. Often just hearing what is going on with someone else gets your mind off of your problems and soon you will find yourself trying to get them to feel better.

Today list the people you think need cheering up and how you will do that:

Name: _____

Cheer up: _____

_____

Name: _____

Cheer up: _____

_____

Name: _____

Cheer up: _____

_____

Six Months Review:

_____

_____

_____

Quotation Source Information:

_____

_____

_____

January 11
July 12

"Your attitude is your most important asset."

Peter Biadasz

We all know people who are a joy to be around or those we avoid based on their most common attitudes. When it comes to your attitude, how do you want people to see you?

_____

_____

What kinds of attitude will you have today and how will you use it to your benefit?

_____

_____

How it will help me today:

_____

_____

_____

Six Months Review:

_____

_____

_____

Quotation Source Information:

_____

_____

_____

January 12
July 13

"We may give without loving,
but we cannot love without giving."

Marilyn S. Possett, L.C.S.W.

Decide what you will give to those you love today. It may be as impressive as a purchased gift or as meaningful as an encouraging word.

Name: _____

Name: _____

Now do it!

Six Months Review:

_____
_____
_____

Quotation Source Information:

_____
_____
_____

January 13
July 14

"Be not angry that you cannot
make others as you wish them to be,
since you cannot make yourself as you wish to be."

Thomas A. Kempis

One of the most common mistakes people make in relationships is trying to change another person into what we think they should be. Accept people as they are and then decide what kind of relationship you want with them. We can only change ourselves.

Are you trying to change someone? Work on accepting them as they are.

Write thoughts here:

_____
_____
_____

Six Months Review:

_____
_____
_____

Quotation Source Information:

_____
_____
_____

January 14
July 15

"When dealing with people,
remember you are not dealing with
creatures of logic, but creatures of emotion."

Dale Carnegie

One of the best tools you can use in nurturing a relationship is acknowledgement. That is the act of letting someone know that you understand what he is feeling. You may not agree with it or be able to figure out why he feels that way but you are only saying, "I understand that is how you feel." This will go a long way in avoiding arguments and letting the other person know that you hear them.

Practice acknowledging someone today. Write the results here:

_____
_____
_____

How good are you at acknowledging others?

_____
_____
_____

Six Months Review:

_____
_____
_____

Quotation Source Information:

_____
_____
_____

January 15
July 16

> "You give but little when you give of your
> possessions. It is when you give of yourself
> that you truly give."

Kahlil Gibran

We all feel good when someone gives to us, even if it is something small. It shows someone that they have an importance to another. Give something of yourself today. It could be a smile, a kind word or an act of generosity:

Name: _____

Gift: _____

_____

Name: _____

Gift: _____

_____

Six Months Review:

_____

_____

_____

Quotation Source Information:

_____

_____

_____

January 16
July 17

"Man is a knot into which relationships are tied."
Antoine de Saint-Exupery

All of us are involved in many, many relationships. Today think about how the relationships in your life affect your life.

Thoughts:

_____
_____
_____

Which are major and which are minor relationships?

Major:

_____
_____

Minor:

_____
_____

Six Months Review:

_____
_____
_____

Quotation Source Information:

_____
_____
_____

January 17
July 18

"Having someone wonder where you are when you don't come home at night is a very old human need."

Margaret Mead

Is there someone in your life who wonders where you are when you don't come home at night?

If so, are you appreciative of them? If not, why not?

Thoughts:

_____
_____
_____

Six Months Review:

_____
_____
_____

Quotation Source Information:

_____
_____
_____

January 18
July 19

"If you want others to be happy practice compassion,
if you want to be happy, practice compassion."

Dalai Lama

Do you regularly show compassion to others? If not, practice until it becomes a regular part of your interaction with others. If you don't know how, seek help from books or others.

What is compassion?

_____

_____

_____

Six Months Review:

_____

_____

_____

Quotation Source Information:

_____

_____

_____

January 19
July 20

"There's one sad truth in life I've found.
While journeying east and west, the only folks we
really wound are those we love the best."

Ella Wheeler Wilcox

Think about those who love you best. Do you treat them as well as you treat strangers or friends? If not, why not?

Thoughts:

_____
_____
_____

Six Months Review:

_____
_____
_____

Quotation Source Information:

_____
_____
_____

January 20
July 21

"If you were going to die soon and had only one phone call you could make, who would you call and what would you say? And why are you waiting?"

Stephen Levine

Call that person today! Tell them what you would like them to know about your relationship.

Name and what I want them to know:

_____
_____
_____

Did you call? _____

Six Months Review:

_____
_____
_____

Quotation Source Information:

_____
_____
_____

January 21
July 22

"Tact is the knack of making a point
without making an enemy."

Isaac Newton

Until we all have the same opinions and feelings there will be conflict.
Think of a conflict you have had recently. How did you handle it? Were
you tactful? Could you have handled it with more tact?

Thoughts:

_____
_____
_____

Six Months Review:

_____
_____
_____

Quotation Source Information:

_____
_____
_____

January 22
July 23

"If you judge people, you have no time to love them."

Mother Teresa

Judging usually occurs when we have incomplete information or a personal bias. Have you ever judged anyone unfairly? Put yourself in their situation. How could you have been more accepting?

Write your thoughts:

_____
_____
_____

Six Months Review:

_____
_____
_____

Quotation Source Information:

_____
_____
_____

January 23
July 24

"Man's best support is a very dear friend."

Cicero

In bad times it is good to have someone to lean on. In good times it is great to have someone to share your joy with. All the time it is best to have someone who you trust to tell you the things that you need to hear, but don't want said. Who is your biggest support person? Have you been as supportive to them? If not, why not?

_____
_____
_____

Six Months Review:

_____
_____
_____

Quotation Source Information:

_____
_____
_____

January 24
July 25

"You can make new friends,
but you can't make old friends."

Martin Amis

Select two old friends and do something special for them today.
Telephone and just say 'Hi,' send them a card with a note of friendship
or send them a basket of fruit.

Name: _____

What I did: _____

_____

Name: _____

What I did: _____

_____

Six Months Review:

_____

_____

_____

Quotation Source Information:

_____

_____

_____

January 25
July 26

> "Always allow your opponents the opportunity
> to walk away from the table with dignity
> because tomorrow they might be your friends."

Willie Brown

It is amazing how people and circumstances can change over time. In relationships you sometimes lose to win, knowing that you will win in the long term. In what circumstances did you use this ploy to strengthen a relationship?

Write it out:

_____
_____
_____

Six Months Review:

_____
_____
_____

Quotation Source Information:

_____
_____
_____

January 26
July 27

> It's not the size of the dog in the fight,
> but the size of the fight in the dog.

Texas Proverb

Relationships, especially long standing relationships, can sometimes be work. But with this work comes depth, in both the relationship as well as the individuals involved. Do you fight to keep your relationships strong? List four things you do to keep them husky and hardy?

1. _____

_____

2. _____

_____

3. _____

_____

4. _____

_____

Six Months Review:

_____

_____

_____

Quotation Source Information:

_____

_____

_____

January 27
July 28

"Give what you have. To someone else it may be better that you dare to think."

Henry Wadsworth Longfellow

Give something of yourself today. It may be a smile, a kind word or deed or it may be money.

Document what you did:

_____

_____

Six Months Review:

_____

_____

_____

Quotation Source Information:

_____

_____

_____

January 28
July 29

"No man succeeds without a good woman behind
him. Wife or mother, if it is both,
he is twice blessed indeed."

Harold MacMillian

Wife or mother, what helpful things has she done to support you? When
is the last time you thanked her?

Helpful support:

_____

_____

_____

Have you thanked her? _____

Six Months Review:

_____

_____

_____

Quotation Source Information:

_____

_____

_____

January 29
July 30

> "My best friends are ones
> who bring out the best in me."

Henry Ford

Who are your best friends? How do they bring out the best in you? Tell them you appreciate that.

Names:
_____
_____

My best qualities:
_____
_____
_____

Six Months Review:
_____
_____
_____

Quotation Source Information:
_____
_____
_____

January 30
July 31

"An insincere and evil friend is more to be feared than a wild beast; a wild beast may wound your body, but an evil friend will wound your mind."

Buddha

Have you ever been wounded by a friend? How did you heal the wound? What did you learn from that experience?

_____
_____
_____

Six Months Review:

_____
_____
_____

Quotation Source Information:

_____
_____
_____

January 31
August 1

"I y'am what I y'am."

Popeye the Sailorman

Sometimes we become rigid and unwilling to change even though what we are doing is harming our relationships. List two things you can change about yourself which will enhance your relationships with others:

1. _____
   _____

2. _____
   _____

Have you changed?

Six Months Review:

_____
_____
_____

Quotation Source Information:

_____
_____
_____

February 1
August 2

"Happy families are all alike.
Unhappy families are all unhappy in their own way."

Leo Tolstoy

Observe a happy family. What things do you notice that seems to make them a happy family unit?

List them:

_____

_____

_____

Six Months Review:

_____

_____

_____

Quotation Source Information:

_____

_____

_____

February 2
August 3

"The meeting of two personalities is like the contact
of two chemical substances: if there is a reaction,
both are transformed."

Carl Jung

In the space below, identify three people who have transformed your life
in a positive way and the way you have been changed. Now tell them and
thank them for their positive influence on you.

1. _____
_____

2. _____
_____

3. _____
_____

Six Months Review:
_____
_____
_____

Quotation Source Information:
_____
_____
_____

February 3
August 4

"What progress, you ask, have I made?
I have begun to be a friend to myself."

Hecato

Sometimes we treat others better than we treat ourselves. Do something for yourself today that you would otherwise do for a friend.

List possibilities here:

_____

_____

_____

Have you made friends with yourself? _____

Six Months Review:

_____

_____

_____

Quotation Source Information:

_____

_____

_____

February 4
August 5

> "The goal in marriage is not to think alike,
> but to think together."

Robert C. Dodds

Have you often tried to change your partner's thinking rather than thinking with him/her together? How well have you been able to think together in your current relationship?

My thoughts:

_____
_____
_____

How have you tried to apply this quote to your relationships? _____

Six Months Review:

_____
_____
_____

Quotation Source Information:

_____
_____
_____

February 5
August 6

"In spite of everything I still believe
that people are really good at heart."

Anne Frank

This is a phenomenal belief statement. If you are not familiar with Anne Frank, look up who she was. Knowing what you do about her, how do you believe she could have made that statement? What are your personal beliefs about this statement?

My thoughts about this quote:

_____
_____
_____
_____

Six Months Review:

_____
_____
_____

Quotation Source Information:

_____
_____
_____

February 6
August 7

"Don't smother each other.
No one can grow in the shade."

Leo Buscaglia

Sometimes our fear of losing someone causes us to hold on tighter which often pushes him or her farther away. List three ways in which you can make certain no one feels smothered in your relationships:

1. _____
   _____

2. _____
   _____

3. _____
   _____

Six Months Review:
_____
_____
_____

Quotation Source Information:
_____
_____
_____

February 7
August 8

"Some people come into our lives and leave footprints on our hearts and we are never ever the same."

Flavia Weedn

Name two people in your life for whom the above quote is true. List what effect they have had on your life. Tell them.

Name: _____

Effect: _____

_____

Name: _____

Effect: _____

_____

What footprints have you left on the lives of others?

Six Months Review:

_____

_____

_____

Quotation Source Information:

_____

_____

_____

February 8
August 9

"You cannot be lonely
if you like the person you're alone with."

Wayne W. Dyer

Relationships are sometimes damaged by one person's efforts to avoid loneliness. Do you like yourself enough to enjoy being alone? Spend some time alone.

Write your thoughts on this:

_____
_____
_____
_____
_____

Six Months Review:

_____
_____
_____

Quotation Source Information:

_____
_____
_____

February 9
August 10

"People change and forget to tell each other."

Lillian Hellman

The only thing that stays the same is that people change. Write down how you have changed in recent years and make a plan to talk about that with your spouse or partner:

Ways I've changed:

_____

_____

_____

My plan to discuss it:

_____

_____

Six Months Review:

_____

_____

_____

Quotation Source Information:

_____

_____

_____

February 10
August 11

"Some of the biggest challenges in relationships come from the fact that most people enter a relationship in order to get something: they're trying to find someone who's going to make them feel good. In reality, the only way a relationship will last is if you see your relationship as a place that you go to give, and not a place that you go to take."

Anthony Robbins

How can you make your relationship more of a place to give rather than to take?

_____
_____
_____
_____

Six Months Review:

_____
_____
_____

Quotation Source Information:

_____
_____
_____

February 11
August 12

"The ultimate test of a relationship is to disagree but hold hands."

Alexandra Penney

Pride, emotions, and incomplete or inaccurate information are but a few of the reasons for disagreements. The next time you have a disagreement with your significant other, hold hands while you are discussing it.

List some times when this is likely to happen:

_____
_____
_____

How did it affect the discussion?

_____
_____
_____

Six Months Review:

_____
_____
_____

Quotation Source Information:

_____
_____
_____

February 12
August 13

"Piglet sidled up to Pooh from behind. 'Pooh!' he whispered. 'Yes, Piglet' 'Nothing,' said Piglet, taking Pooh's paw. 'I just wanted to be sure of you.'"

A.A. Milne

Often there is comfort just being with someone, even if you are not talking. List the name of the person who gives you comfort simply by their presence. Let them know how you feel.

My plan:

_____
_____
_____
_____
_____

Six Months Review:

_____
_____
_____

Quotation Source Information:

_____
_____
_____

February 13
August 14

"You can kiss your family and friends good-bye and put miles between you, but at the same time you carry them with you in your heart, your mind, your stomach, because you do not just live in a world but a world lives in you."

Frederick Buechner

List the ways in which who you are today is directly related to the family you grew up in and the friends you had as a child. How do these things affect your important relationships?

_____
_____
_____
_____
_____

Six Months Review:

_____
_____
_____

Quotation Source Information:

_____
_____
_____

February 14
August 15

"Valentine's Day is for lovers and those we love."

Marilyn S. Possett, L.C.S.W.

It is Valentine's Day. Which special people will you acknowledge today?

_____

_____

And how: _____

Six Months Review:

_____

_____

_____

Quotation Source Information:

_____

_____

_____

February 15
August 16

"If we are incapable of finding peace in ourselves,
it is pointless to search elsewhere."

Francois de la Rochefoucauld

How do you feel about the peace you have within yourself?

_____

_____

_____

What are the areas of conflict?

_____

_____

_____

How can the conflict be resolved?

_____

_____

_____

Six Months Review:

_____

_____

_____

Quotation Source Information:

_____

_____

_____

February 16
August 17

"The success of a relationship is a function of the extent to which it meets the needs of two people."

Phillip C. McGraw

Maybe he needs words of encouragement or she needs a hug a day. Do you know what your partner's needs are? Write them here. Do one thing today to meet those needs.

My partner's needs:

_____
_____
_____

What will I do today?

_____
_____

Six Months Review:

_____
_____
_____

Quotation Source Information:

_____
_____
_____

February 17
August 18

"If you want to make peace, you don't talk to your friends, you talk to your enemies."

Moshe Dayan

List three people you consider your enemies. Formulate a solution to the issues at hand and develop a strategy to begin a lifetime of peace in each relationship. When you are ready, make it happen.

Name: _____
Solution: _____
_____

Name: _____
Solution: _____
_____

Name: _____
Solution: _____
_____

Six Months Review:
_____
_____
_____

Quotation Source Information:
_____
_____
_____

February 18
August 19

"If what you are doing in your relationship is not working, do something different."

Michele Weiner-Davis

Examine what is not working in one of your relationships. Do you always argue about the same things? Do you continually get upset with your partner or spouse about the same thing? Try reacting differently in these situations.

Below list what you are going to do differently in your relationship:

_____
_____
_____
_____

Six Months Review:

_____
_____
_____

Quotation Source Information:

_____
_____
_____

February 19
August 20

"Always communicate as if you are moving a couch with someone you cannot see. You will need to be very clear about what you are saying to get where you want to go."

John D. Hurlburt, Ph.D.

After being in a relationship for a while we may begin to think the other person always knows what we mean when we speak. How clear are you when communicating with your partner or spouse? List three ways you will practice being clearer in your communication:

1. _____
   _____

2. _____
   _____

3. _____
   _____

Six Months Review:

_____
_____
_____

Quotation Source Information:

_____
_____
_____

February 20
August 21

"Children require guidance and sympathy
far more than instruction."

Annie Sullivan

List ways as a child you were shown guidance and sympathy rather than instruction:

1. _____
   _____

2. _____
   _____

3. _____
   _____

Indicate above who provided these experiences to you.

How can you pass this wisdom on to your children or other significant people in your life?

_____
_____
_____

Six Months Review:

_____
_____
_____

Quotation Source Information:

_____
_____
_____

February 21
August 22

"Caring partners converse in a caring way."

Willard F. Harley, Jr

What are conversations like with your partner? Are you often critical and impatient or caring and kind? Below write out how you will greet your partner when you get home tonight:

_____
_____
_____

Six Months Review:

_____
_____
_____

Quotation Source Information:

_____
_____
_____

"Relationships are difficult,
but we can't live without them."

Dian S. Dowell, L.P.C.

We are in many, many relationships throughout our lives, from business to personal, to intimate. Managing them can be a challenge. Try to look from the point of view of the other person when there is a conflict.

Think of someone with whom you are having a difficult relationship. What is their point of view? Write it down.

Name: _____

Their view:
_____
_____
_____

Six Months Review:
_____
_____
_____

Quotation Source Information:
_____
_____
_____

February 23
August 24

"When men and women are able to respect and accept their differences then love has a chance to blossom."

John Gray, Ph.D.

Who is the one who has to be right in your relationship? Try to think in terms of differences rather than right and wrong.

_____

_____

What do you and your partner argue about the most? Write it here.

_____

_____

Is there a chance that this disagreement could be settled by simply accepting the differences between you? Make it happen.

My plan:

_____

_____

_____

Have you accepted your partner's differences? _____

Six Months Review:

_____

_____

_____

Quotation Source Information:

_____

_____

_____

February 24
August 25

> "No one can whistle a symphony.
> It takes an orchestra to play it."

H.E. Luccock

Every person plays a different yet vital role in a relationship. List ways you play a vital role in the relationships in which you are involved:

1. _____

   _____

2. _____

   _____

3. _____

   _____

Six Months Review:

_____

_____

_____

Quotation Source Information:

_____

_____

_____

February 25
August 26

"When I was a boy of fourteen, my father was so ignorant I could hardly stand to have the old man around. But when I got to be twenty-one, I was astonished at how much the old man had learned in those seven years."

Mark Twain

Whether we had a good or poor childhood there are things we learned from our fathers. List some:

_____

_____

_____

If possible, tell your father what positive things you have learned from him.

Six Months Review:

_____

_____

_____

Quotation Source Information:

_____

_____

_____

February 26
August 27

"Nothing you do for your children is ever wasted. They seem not to notice us, hovering, averting our eyes, and they seldom offer thanks, but what we do for them is never wasted."

Garrison Keillor

Children learn about relationships through observation. If you have children, what are they learning from you? What do you want them to learn? Is there one improvement you could make? List below:

_____
_____
_____

Six Months Review:

_____
_____
_____

Quotation Source Information:

_____
_____
_____

February 27
August 28

"Never go to bed mad. Stay up and fight."

Phyllis Diller

Well, instead of fighting, resolve the issue before bedtime. You will sleep much better. Have you ever gone to bed angry with your partner? If so, what could you do differently next time? Write below:

_____
_____
_____

Six Months Review:

_____
_____
_____

Quotation Source Information:

_____
_____
_____

February 28
August 29

"People most often change
when they don't feel they have to."

Afflatus

Are you continually trying to change someone into doing what you think they should do? If so, make a plan to stop trying to change them and allow them to be their own person. You may be surprised at the outcome. Write your plan here:

_____
_____
_____

Six Months Review:

_____
_____
_____

Quotation Source Information:

_____
_____
_____

February 29
August 30

"When raising your children you have the
opportunity to be raising your future best friends."

Marilyn S. Possett, L.C.S.W.

Think about what kind of friend you prefer. What are the qualities of a good friend? Are you modeling these for your children? It is a wonderful gift when our adult children are also our friends.

Qualities:

_____
_____
_____

Feelings:

_____
_____
_____

Six Months Review:

_____
_____
_____

Quotation Source Information:

_____
_____
_____

March 1
August 31

"Manners maketh man."

William of Wykeham

First impressions are very important. What do your manners say about you? Is there something you need to work on? Write it here:

_____

_____

_____

Six Months Review:

_____

_____

_____

Quotation Source Information:

_____

_____

_____

March 2
September 1

"Life is about becoming more than we are."

Oprah Winfrey

In other words be more than you think you can be. List five of your positive character traits. In the next six months, how are you going to make them better?

1. _____

_____

2. _____

_____

3. _____

_____

4. _____

_____

5. _____

_____

Six Months Review:

_____

_____

_____

Quotation Source Information:

_____

_____

_____

March 3
September 2

"It is not what they take away from you that counts:
it's what you do with what you have left."

Hubert H. Humphrey

Losses are often difficult and we tend to focus on the loss rather than on what is left. What are the most significant losses in your life? What do you have left? What did you gain from these experiences?

_____
_____
_____
_____
_____

Six Months Review:

_____
_____
_____

Quotation Source Information:

_____
_____
_____

March 4
September 3

> "It doesn't matter who my father was;
> it matters who I remember he was."

Anne Sexton

How you remember your parents will shape how you view yourself. List three things that you remember about each of your parents and how that has affected you:

Your father:

1. _____

   _____

2. _____

   _____

3. _____

   _____

Your mother:

1. _____

   _____

2. _____

   _____

3. _____

   _____

Six Months Review:

_____

_____

_____

Quotation Source Information:

_____

_____

_____

March 5
September 4

"You don't live in a world all your own.
Your brothers are here, too."

Albert Schweitzer

In the past 24 hours how many people have you encountered either in person, by phone, e-mail, etc.? _____

Register ways that you acknowledge others on a daily basis:

1. _____
   _____

2. _____
   _____

3. _____
   _____

Six Months Review:

_____
_____
_____

Quotation Source Information:

_____
_____
_____

March 6
September 5

"What, me worry?"

Alfred E. Neuman

Stress, not managed well, can adversely affect any relationship. How do you manage stress? List six things you can do to alleviate the effects of stress:

1. _____

   _____

2. _____

   _____

3. _____

   _____

4. _____

   _____

5. _____

   _____

6. _____

   _____

Practice them!!!

Six Months Review:

_____

_____

_____

Quotation Source Information:

_____

_____

_____

March 7
September 6

"Go ahead, make my day."

Harry Callahan

Today, perform three spontaneous random acts of kindness to try to make someone's day special. List what you did here:

1. _____

   _____

2. _____

   _____

3. _____

   _____

4. _____

   _____

5. _____

   _____

Six Months Review:

_____

_____

_____

Quotation Source Information:

_____

_____

_____

March 8
September 7

"Hey, dude, let's party!"

Jeff Spicolli

Relationships are hard work. Choose 10 of the most important relationships you are involved in and invite these people to a party. Make your relationships fun.

Party plans:

_____

_____

_____

_____

_____

_____

Plan another party in six months.

Six Months Review:

_____

_____

_____

Quotation Source Information:

_____

_____

_____

March 9
September 8

> "A good relationship is like a garden.
> If you nurture it and care for it, it grows.
> If you neglect it, it withers and dies."

Marilyn S. Possett, L.C.S.W.

What is the most important relationship in your life? How will you care for your relationship garden today? List some things you can do:

Relationship with: _____

How can I nurture it today?

_____
_____
_____
_____
_____
_____

Six Months Review:

_____
_____
_____

Quotation Source Information:

_____
_____
_____

March 10
September 9

"Kind words can be short and easy to speak,
but their echoes are truly endless."

Mother Teresa

Words, once spoken cannot be taken back. Make sure your words echo with kindness. Think about this today and write your thoughts here:

_____
_____
_____

Six Months Review:

_____
_____
_____

Quotation Source Information:

_____
_____
_____

March 11
September 10

> "If you wish to make a man your enemy,
> tell him simply, 'You are wrong.'
> This method works every time."

Unknown

It is not what we say but often the way we say it that sparks a defensive reaction from others. Maybe there is a more tactful way to communicate. Think before you speak. How well do you use tact in your relationships?

Here is an area I need to work on:

_____
_____
_____

Six Months Review:

_____
_____
_____

March 12
September 11

> "Sticks and stones are hard on bones
> Aimed with angry art,
> Words can sting like anything
> But silence breaks the heart."

Suzanne Nichols

One of the three major behaviors that can hurt a relationship is withdrawal. Sometimes it is used to avoid conflict and sometimes it is used to punish. Just being silent speaks volumes. Examine your style of conflict resolution. Is withdrawal any part of it? Write your thoughts here:

_____
_____
_____
_____
_____

Six Months Review:

_____
_____
_____

Quotation Source Information:

_____
_____
_____

March 13
September 12

"The number one cause for the breakdown in marriages in our country is that people don't spend enough time together."

Michele Weiner Davis

When is the last time you spent time alone with your special friends and/or lover? Plan regular get-togethers with someone special. You don't have to spend money: you can take a walk, read out loud or just talk together for 15 minutes a day. Write your plan here:

_____
_____
_____
_____
_____

Six Months Review:

_____
_____
_____

Quotation Source Information:

_____
_____
_____

March 14
September 13

"The art of being wise
is the art of knowing what to overlook."

William James

Every person has good and not as good qualities. Relationships go well when we pay attention to the good and overlook the rest. What things will you overlook in your most important relationships?

_____

_____

_____

_____

_____

Six Months Review:

_____

_____

_____

Quotation Source Information:

_____

_____

_____

March 15
September 14

Churning water, for however long a time,
does not produce butter.

Buddhist Proverb

We know that one definition of insanity is doing the same thing over and over and expecting different results. Do you keep going over the same things in your relationships and nothing changes? If so, what can you do differently?

_____

_____

_____

_____

_____

Six Months Review:

_____

_____

Quotation Source Information:

_____

_____

_____

March 16
September 15

"Kindness is loving people more than they deserve."

Joseph Joubert

We have all had instances when we were treated better than we thought we should have been. Record ways you have shown extraordinary kindness to others:

_____

_____

_____

_____

_____

Six Months Review:

_____

_____

_____

Quotation Source Information:

_____

_____

_____

March 17
September 16

"Learn to love the one person who will absolutely be with you for the rest of your life—*yourself.*"

Cherie Carter-Scott

It has been said that we have to be happy with ourselves before we can be in a healthy relationship. Then a good relationship is an extra goodie in life. What do you like about yourself? Write down your individual strengths. Also write down your weaknesses. Work to make them strengths, and believe in yourself.

Strengths:

_____
_____
_____

Weaknesses:

_____
_____
_____

Six Months Review:

_____
_____
_____

Quotation Source Information:

_____
_____
_____

March 18
September 17

"The best portion of a good life is the little nameless, unremembered acts of kindness and love."

William Wordsworth

We all feel great when someone does something good for us. Especially when it is unexpected. It can be fun and very rewarding to provide someone with an anonymous act of kindness. Do this today! Record the experience on the lines below.

_____
_____
_____
_____
_____

Six Months Review:

_____
_____
_____

Quotation Source Information:

_____
_____
_____

March 19
September 18

"No human relation gives one possession in another—every two souls are absolutely different. In friendship or in love, the two side by side raise hands together to find what one cannot reach alone."

Kahlil Gibran

Working as a team a relationship can be well balanced. Each person uses the strengths he has for the good of the team. What three talents or strengths do you bring to your most important personal relationship?

1. _____
   _____

2. _____
   _____

3. _____
   _____

What are your partner's strengths? How do they make the sum greater than the parts?

_____
_____
_____
_____

Six Months Review:

_____
_____

Quotation Source Information:

_____
_____
_____

March 20
September 19

"Recipe for having friends: BE ONE!"

Elbert Hubbard

There have been many definitions of friendship. Write yours. Are you cooking with that recipe?

_____

_____

_____

_____

_____

Six Months Review:

_____

_____

_____

Quotation Source Information:

_____

_____

_____

March 21
September 20

"Appreciative words are the most powerful force
for good on earth."

George W. Crane

Appreciation is one of the most important ingredients in a healthy relationship. When someone doesn't feel appreciated, resentment often fol-
lows. Sometimes we forget to show appreciation. Today, work on showing
appreciation to others. Record the experience on the lines below.

_____

_____

_____

_____

_____

Six Months Review:

_____

_____

_____

Quotation Source Information:

_____

_____

_____

March 22
September 21

"A strong, positive self-image
is the best possible preparation for success in life."

Joyce Brothers

Do you have the habit of *beating yourself up* over some personal weakness or limitation? If so, examine your so-called weaknesses. Are they hurting you? If they are, make a plan to stop beating yourself up and make some changes.

_____

_____

_____

_____

_____

Six Months Review:

_____

_____

_____

Quotation Source Information:

_____

_____

_____

March 23
September 22

"Any fact facing us is not as important as our attitude
toward it, for that determines our success or failure."

Norman Vincent Peale

Our thoughts determine our feelings about a situation. Make sure your thoughts are not distorted but are based in reality. That will determine your attitude and, therefore, your success. Write a situation you are dealing with and your thoughts about it.

_____
_____
_____
_____
_____

Six Months Review:

_____
_____
_____

Quotation Source Information:

_____
_____
_____

March 24
September 23

"When the one Great Scorer comes to write against
your name, He marks not that you won or lost but
how you played the game."

Grantland Rice

History is full of people of great and small accomplishment. But rarely
does history deeply examine the character traits that made the person.
Which is more important to you and how do you want to be remembered? Write your epitaph here:

_____
_____
_____
_____
_____

Six Months Review:

_____
_____
_____

Quotation Source Information:

_____
_____
_____

March 25
September 24

"In spite of illness, in spite even of the archenemy of sorrow, one can remain alive long past the usual date of disintegration if one is unafraid to change, insatiable in intellectual curiosity, interested in big things, and happy in small ways."

Edith Wharton

Sometimes we hold fast to our way of thinking and doing because if we can convince others that we are right, it validates us. Being unafraid to make changes in ourselves is a very important ingredient in being able to enjoy life. Along with remaining curious and interested, look for joy in the small things and be thankful.

Look at the quote above. Do you know someone who lives his or her life this way? Tell them you admire them.

_____
_____
_____

Six Months Review:

_____
_____
_____

Quotation Source Information:

_____
_____
_____

March 26
September 25

"Laughter gives us distance. It allows us to step back
from an event, deal with it and then move on."

Bob Newhart

One of the most underused senses we have is our sense of humor. Using
it can make lighter even the heaviest load. Think of an example when
you could have used a lighter moment. Now plan ways to fine-tune your
sense of humor. Read humorous material, send funny cards, and practice on your friends and family. Write thoughts below:

_____

_____

_____

_____

_____

Six Months Review:

_____

_____

_____

Quotation Source Information:

_____

_____

_____

March 27
September 26

> "Call it a clan, call it a network,
> call it a tribe, call it a family:
> Whatever you call it, whoever you are, you need one."

Jane Howard

Not everyone has a supportive family. If you have no family, if you have no tribe, if you have no clan, you can still create a network of support for yourself. Many people have good friends whom they consider family. Who is in your support network? If you don't have one, get started on creating one today.

_____
_____
_____
_____
_____

Six Months Review:

_____
_____
_____

Quotation Source Information:

_____
_____
_____

March 28
September 27

"Don't make another's problem yours. If in doubt, ask yourself: Whose problem is this and do I have any control over the solution?"

Marilyn S. Possett, L.C.S.W.

Just because someone talks to you about their problem does not mean you have to solve it for them. Sometimes they just need to talk about it until they find their own solution.

Whose problems are you involved in today? How will you let their problems go?

_____

_____

_____

Six Months Review:

_____

_____

_____

Quotation Source Information:

_____

_____

_____

March 29
September 28

"The most remarkable thing about my mother is that for thirty years she served the family nothing but leftovers. The original meal has never been found."

Calvin Trillin

Remember your mother's cooking? Whether it was good or bad was it done with love? Call your mother today and thank her for feeding you for all those years.

_____
_____
_____

Six Months Review:
_____
_____
_____

Quotation Source Information:
_____
_____
_____

March 30
September 29

"I have found the best way to give advice to your children is to find out what they want and then advise them to do it."

Harry Truman

Rather than just giving advice to your children, listen to them and discover what they want. Then you can help them find out how to get it. Practice asking questions with your children rather than offering advice. Write a plan here:

_____
_____
_____
_____
_____

Six Months Review:

_____
_____
_____

Quotation Source Information:

_____
_____
_____

March 31
September 30

"Opportunity is missed by most people because it comes dressed in overalls and looks like work."

Thomas Edison

Despite what is portrayed on television and in the movies, a healthy relationship takes hard work. You have the opportunity to experience good relationships in your life if you look at them as opportunities instead of work. How can you work hard on your relationships?

_____
_____
_____
_____
_____

Six Months Review:

_____
_____
_____

Quotation Source Information:

_____
_____
_____

April 1
October 1

"Even if you're on the right track,
you'll get run over if you just sit there."

Will Rogers

In relationships, as in life, doing nothing is doing something. When confronted in a relationship, have you ever said, "I didn't do anything"? Pick one relationship and do something today to improve it. Write your plan here:

_____
_____
_____
_____
_____

Six Months Review:

_____
_____
_____

Quotation Source Information:

_____
_____
_____

April 2
October 2

"You do not really understand something
unless you can explain it to your grandmother."

Albert Einstein

When we are trying to explain our position or point of view to someone it is easy to become impatient if we think they do not understand. Sometimes we raise our voice hoping that will help them to get it. Examine the feeling. Usually we feel frustrated at our lack of ability to explain ourselves. Next time you have to explain something, take a deep breath and slow down. It will help. Write your thoughts here:

_____
_____
_____
_____
_____

Six Months Review:

_____
_____
_____

Quotation Source Information:

_____
_____
_____

April 3
October 3

"We must be willing to get rid of the life we've planned, so as to have the life that is waiting for us."

Joseph Campbell

When life doesn't turn out the way we planned we may think we have failed. However, it is not so much failure as trying some things that did not work. Every door that closes allows us to open another. Be open to see what is inside. Write what you thought you would be doing at this point in your life. Is it what you are doing?

_____

_____

_____

_____

_____

Six Months Review:

_____

_____

_____

Quotation Source Information:

_____

_____

_____

April 4
October 4

> "The thing that you were attracted to in a person often turns out to be what annoys you the most."

Sydney Nelson-Hunt, L.C.S.W.

As odd as that may seem, it is very often true. For example, if you were attracted to someone's spontaneity in the beginning, after awhile it may seem more like irresponsibility and impulsiveness. Think about what attracted you to your spouse or partner. Do you still like that quality about him/her? Write it here:

_____
_____
_____
_____
_____

Six Months Review:

_____
_____
_____

Quotation Source Information:

_____
_____
_____

April 5
October 5

"When my kids become wild and unruly, I use a nice, safe playpen. When they're finished, I climb out."

Erma Bombeck

Raising children is a rewarding, and yet, an exhausting job. Be sure to take a timeout when you are feeling overwhelmed. Plan some mini-breaks throughout the day and regularly plan some time away from them. You will return refreshed and renewed. Plan your breaks here:

_____
_____
_____
_____
_____

Six Months Review:

_____
_____
_____

Quotation Source Information:

_____
_____
_____

April 6
October 6

"No one like one's mother and father ever lived."

Robert Lowell

Think about it, everyone of us is unique in our own way. What is unique about your parents? Write it here. If appropriate, tell them.

_____
_____
_____

Six Months Review:

_____
_____
_____

Quotation Source Information:

_____
_____
_____

April 7
October 7

ATTITUDE

"The remarkable thing is we have a choice every day regarding the attitude we will embrace for that day. We cannot change our past…we cannot change the fact that people will act in a certain way. We cannot change the inevitable. The only thing we can do is play on the one string we have, and that is our attitude…

I am convinced that life is 10% what happens to me and 90% how I react to it.
And so it is with you…we are in charge of our Attitudes."

Charles Swindoll

How would you describe your attitude?

_____
_____
_____

How would those in your closest relationships describe your attitude?

_____
_____
_____

Record some ways that you can improve your attitude:

_____
_____
_____

Six Months Review:

_____

_____

_____

Quotation Source Information:

_____

_____

_____

April 8
October 8

> "Facts do not cease to exist
> because they are ignored."

Carl W. Buechner

Sometimes we try to ignore things in our relationships that bother us. But stuffing them down often causes resentment and produces no changes. Choose the ones that cause the most distress and deal with them.

List the facts about your relationships that you have ignored:

_____

_____

_____

Begin to resolve each today.

Six Months Review:

_____

_____

_____

Quotation Source Information:

_____

_____

_____

April 9
October 9

"Teamwork is the ability to work together
toward a common vision. The ability to
direct individual accomplishments toward
organizational objectives. It is the fuel that
allows common people to attain uncommon results."

Andrew Carnegie

If each person does what they do best in a relationship it can be a successful team. Utilizing everyone's strengths makes for a healthy relationship.

List the ways you develop teamwork in relationships:

_____
_____
_____
_____
_____

Six Months Review:

_____
_____
_____

Quotation Source Information:

_____
_____
_____

April 10
October 10

"It is amazing how much you can accomplish when it doesn't matter who gets the credit."

Unknown

This relates to yesterday's quote on teamwork. In a successful relationship the team gets the credit. Have you been guilty of needing more credit than you deserved? _____

Write your thoughts about the above quote here:

_____
_____
_____
_____
_____

Six Months Review:

_____
_____
_____

April 11
October 11

"Wearing the same shirts doesn't make you a team."

Buchholz and Roth

Many people are related by blood but not by daily relationship. They are complete strangers to each other even though they may share the same last name. However, there are other families that are very close. List three families you know that exemplify what teamwork is all about:

1. _____
   _____

2. _____
   _____

3. _____
   _____

How do they develop the teamwork you have observed? Note your answer above.

Six Months Review:
_____
_____
_____

Quotation Source Information:
_____
_____
_____

April 12
October 12

> ## "Synergy—the bonus that is achieved when things work together harmoniously"

Mark Twain

When all the right elements and people get together at the right time, the power of two can produce the results of many. What is your definition of synergy?

_____
_____
_____

How have you achieved synergy in past relationships?

_____
_____
_____

How can you synergize your existing relationships?

_____
_____
_____

Six Months Review:

_____
_____
_____

Quotation Source Information:

_____
_____
_____

April 13
October 13

"Without forgiveness,
there can be no real freedom to act within a group."

Max DePree

Lack of forgiveness from current as well as past relationships can affect current as well as future relationships. List any unforgiven things that you are holding onto from current or previous relationships:

_____
_____
_____
_____
_____

Contact each party, if possible and appropriate, to extend forgiveness. Record the process in the space above.

Six Months Review:

_____
_____
_____

Quotation Source Information:

_____
_____
_____

April 14
October 14

"Men are motivated and empowered
when they feel needed. Women are motivated and
empowered when they feel cherished."

John Gray, Ph.D.

Men and women have differing and various needs in their relationships.
Look at your relationship from your partner's view. How are you helping your partner feel needed or cherished?

_____

_____

_____

Six Months Review:

_____

_____

_____

Quotation Source Information:

_____

_____

_____

April 15
October 15

"If you cannot get rid of the family skeleton,
you may as well make it dance."

George Bernard Shaw

It is time to clean out the closet and throw away the skeleton and the skeleton key. How can you turn negative family background into positives?

1. _____

   _____

2. _____

   _____

3. _____

   _____

Six Months Review:

_____
_____
_____

Quotation Source Information:

_____
_____
_____

April 16
October 16

> "If you want to achieve your full potential,
> assist another in achieving theirs."

Peter Biadasz

When you help others you are also helping yourself. What does the above quote mean to you?

_____

_____

_____

_____

_____

Six Months Review:

_____

_____

_____

Quotation Source Information:

_____

_____

_____

April 17
October 17

"The simplest toy, one which even the youngest child can operate, is called a grandparent."

Sam Levenson

Grandparents can have all the fun with the grandchildren without the burden of responsibility…or can they? Either way, each grandparent will showcase the positive of each parent.

List three childhood memories of your grandparents:

1. _____
   _____

2. _____
   _____

3. _____
   _____

How can you utilize those memories to positively influence others?

_____
_____
_____

Six Months Review:

_____
_____
_____

Quotation Source Information:

_____
_____
_____

April 18
October 18

"It's not stress that kills us, it is our reaction to it."

Hans Selye

The effects of stress on our bodies may be physical, such as headaches or back pain; or stress can affect us emotionally such as when we become more irritable or are unable to sleep. It is in our best interest to manage stress effectively. Record the ways you relieve stress:

_____

_____

_____

_____

_____

Six Months Review:

_____

_____

_____

Quotation Source Information:

_____

_____

_____

April 19
October 19

"Actions, not words, are the true criterion of the attachment of friends."

George Washington

Watch the actions of others. Do they match their words? Do yours? How do others show their friendship to you by their actions?

_____

_____

_____

How do your actions convey friendship to others?

_____

_____

_____

Six Months Review:

_____

_____

_____

Quotation Source Information:

_____

_____

_____

April 20
October 20

"Children seldom misquote you. In fact, they usually repeat word for word what you shouldn't have said."

Unknown

We have all seen children imitate their parents. My parents have great stories of when they were imitated, but for the wrong behavior or speech. What are some of your parent's often used quotes?

_____

_____

_____

Which do you, will you or have you used with your children?

_____

_____

_____

List three quotes that you want your children to utilize when quoting you:

1. _____

_____

2. _____

_____

3. _____

_____

Start the teaching process today, not just to children, but to everyone with whom you come in contact with.

Six Months Review:

_____

_____

_____

April 21
October 21

> "If we had no winter,
> the spring would not be so pleasant:
> if we did not sometimes taste of adversity,
> prosperity would not be so welcome."

Anne Bradstreet

We can learn to have better relationships by the adversity that we walk through. List the things you have learned through adversity, which have resulted in better relationships for you.

_____
_____
_____
_____
_____

Six Months Review:

_____
_____
_____

Quotation Source Information:

_____
_____
_____

April 22
October 22

"If you want to be respected by others the great thing is to respect yourself. Only by that, only by self-respect will you compel others to respect you."

Fyodor Dostoevsky

Define respect:

_____

_____

How do you feel about the way you respect yourself?

_____

_____

List the ways you can improve your self-respect:

1. _____

_____

2. _____

_____

3. _____

_____

Begin this growth process today.

Six Months Review:

_____

_____

_____

Quotation Source Information:

_____

_____

_____

April 23
October 23

"Honest disagreement is often a good sign of progress."

Mahatma Gandhi

If someone disagrees with you, is your initial reaction to become tense? Their opinion does not make you wrong, just different. Acknowledging that is a big step in resolving disagreements. How can you have honest and healthy disagreements?

_____

_____

_____

_____

_____

Six Months Review:

_____

_____

_____

Quotation Source Information:

_____

_____

_____

April 24
October 24

"People who cannot find time for recreation are
obliged sooner or later to find time for illness."

John Wanamaker

How do you find times for rest and relaxation?

_____

_____

_____

Do you rest and relax enough?   _____

What do you do to rest and relax?

_____

_____

_____

Six Months Review:

_____

_____

_____

Quotation Source Information:

_____

_____

_____

April 25
October 25

> "A man who doesn't trust himself can
> never really trust anyone else."

Cardinal De Retz

Until we really get to know someone, we have a tendency to view others as we view ourselves. If we cannot trust ourselves, we usually feel that others are untrustworthy. Do you trust yourself in all situations?

_____

How does that affect your relationships?

_____
_____
_____

How can you improve your self-trust level?

_____
_____
_____

Six Months Review:

_____
_____
_____

Quotation Source Information:

_____
_____
_____

April 26
October 26

"After all this is over, all that will really have mattered
is how we treated each other."

Unknown

Generally speaking, are you pleased with the way you treat others?

_____

List some ways you can treat others in your life better:

_____
_____
_____
_____
_____

Six Months Review:

_____
_____
_____

April 27
October 27

"If the world seems cold to you,
kindle fires to warm it."

David Lloyd George

Think about ways you can warm the world around you and fire up your
relationships:

_____
_____
_____
_____
_____

Carry out your plan.

Six Months Review:

_____
_____
_____

Quotation Source Information:

_____
_____
_____

April 28
October 28

"It isn't a lack of love, but a lack of friendship that makes unhappy marriages."

Friedrich Nietzshe

Many successful couples have said that the strongest part of their marriage is their friendship to each other. List examples of friendship in marriages you have observed:

_____
_____
_____

How can these examples translate into your primary relationship?

_____
_____
_____

Six Months Review:

_____
_____
_____

Quotation Source Information:

_____
_____
_____

April 29
October 29

"They may forget what you said, but they will never forget how you made them feel."

Carl W. Buechner

List three people that made you feel great about yourself:

1. _____
   _____

2. _____
   _____

3. _____
   _____

How did they do it? Do the same for others in your life.

Six Months Review:

_____
_____
_____

Quotation Source Information:

_____
_____
_____

April 30
October 30

"You cannot shake hands with a clenched fist."

Indira Gandhi

Many times when we are angry, we wait for the other person to take the initiative to heal the situation. How do you open yourself to others even when angry?

_____

_____

_____

_____

_____

Can anger be used constructively in relationships? _____
Why or why not?

_____

_____

_____

Six Months Review:

_____

_____

_____

Quotation Source Information:

_____

_____

_____

May 1
October 31

"Love the heart that hurts you,
but never hurt the heart that loves you."

Vipin Sharma

We have all been hurt while in love. How can we always show love to the heart that may have hurt us?

_____
_____
_____

Six Months Review:

_____
_____
_____

Quotation Source Information:

_____
_____
_____

May 2
November 1

"How much more grievous are the consequences of anger than the causes of it."

Marcus Aurelius

It is easy to note the consequences of reacting in anger. List ways to constructively respond to anger:

_____

_____

_____

What are the differences between responding and reacting?

_____

_____

_____

Six Months Review:

_____

_____

_____

Quotation Source Information:

_____

_____

_____

May 3
November 2

"Until you make peace with who you are,
you'll never be content with what you have."

Doris Mortman

Are you at peace with yourself and who you are? _____

If not, how can you be more peaceful with yourself?

_____
_____
_____

Six Months Review:

_____
_____
_____

Quotation Source Information:

_____
_____
_____

May 4
November 3

"To carry a grudge is like being stung to death by one bee."

William Walton

Have you been harboring feelings of resentment toward someone?

_____

Maybe it is time to let go for your own sake. List any grudges you are carrying:

1. _____
   _____

2. _____
   _____

3. _____
   _____

Next to each grudge listed write how you will begin to resolve each today.

Six Months Review:

_____
_____
_____

Quotation Source Information:

_____
_____
_____

May 5
November 4

"If anything terrifies me, I must try to conquer it."

Francis Charles Chichester

We all have fears of some sort. What things terrify you the most in relationships?

_____

_____

_____

_____

_____

Which is your biggest fear? _____

Write a plan to overcome each of those fears:

_____

_____

_____

_____

_____

Six Months Review:

_____

_____

_____

Quotation Source Information:

_____

_____

_____

May 6
November 5

"We must be willing to let go of the life we have
planned, so as to have the life that is waiting for us."

E.M. Forest

People go into relationships with expectations. Sometimes both people
have different expectations. List all the expectations that you have for
your most precious relationships:

_____
_____
_____
_____
_____

How can those expectations get in the way of the relationship reaching
its fullest potential?

_____
_____
_____
_____
_____

Six Months Review:

_____
_____

Quotation Source Information:

_____
_____
_____

May 7
November 6

"As is our confidence, so is our capacity."

William Hazlitt

Baggage from past relationship can have an effect on our confidence in future relationships. List all of your known baggage from past relationships:

_____
_____
_____
_____
_____

Write action plans to deal with each item listed and reap the rewards of greater confidence in your relationships:

_____
_____
_____
_____
_____

Six Months Review:

_____
_____
_____

Quotation Source Information:

_____
_____
_____

May 8
November 7

"Forgiveness is a gift you give yourself. It does not change the past, but it certainly changes the future."

Ramona S. Moody, L.C.S.W.

Holding a grudge only hurts the grudge-holder. Often the other person is not thinking about what happened at all. Forgiving is not the same as forgetting. Forgiving allows you to get unstuck, quit being consumed by what happened and move on. Is there someone you need to forgive today for your own sake?

_____
_____
_____

Six Months Review:

_____
_____
_____

Quotation Source Information:

_____
_____
_____

May 9
November 8

"In the middle of difficulty lies opportunity."

Albert Einstein

A difficulty is nothing more than an opportunity in disguise. List a recent relationship difficulty and the opportunity that arose as a result:

_____
_____
_____
_____
_____

When future difficulties arise, look for the opportunity that is in hiding.

Six Months Review:

_____
_____
_____

Quotation Source Information:

_____
_____
_____

May 10
November 9

"Each person must live their life as a model for others."

Rosa Parks

We often learn about relationships by observing others. Who are your relationship role models?

_____

_____

_____

What characteristics or behaviors do you admire about them?

_____

_____

_____

In what ways did they serve as models for you?

_____

_____

_____

How can you serve as a model for others?

_____

_____

_____

Six Months Review:

_____

_____

_____

Quotation Source Information:

_____

_____

_____

May 11
November 10

"Kindness is a language
the deaf can hear and the blind can see."

Mark Twain

Do you know someone who is always kind to others? Ask him/her about
that. Write your thoughts here.

_____
_____
_____
_____
_____

Six Months Review:

_____
_____
_____

Quotation Source Information:

_____
_____
_____

May 12
November 11

"High expectations are the key to everything."

Sam Walton

The higher the expectations, the better the results. How could expecting more from yourself or others improve your relationships?

_____

_____

_____

List constructive ways you can raise the expectation level in your primary relationships:

_____

_____

_____

_____

_____

Six Months Review:

_____

_____

_____

Quotation Source Information:

_____

_____

_____

May 13
November 12

"Teamwork: Simply stated, it is less me and more we."

Unknown

What is your definition of teamwork?

_____
_____
_____

How does your definition of teamwork add value to your relationships?

_____
_____
_____

Six Months Review:

_____
_____
_____

May 14
November 13

"No person has ever been honored for what he received. Honor has been the reward for what he gave."

Calvin Coolidge

If you were to hand out three awards for "Giving in a Relationship", who would you give them to and why?

1. _____
   _____

2. _____
   _____

3. _____
   _____

Contact these three people, express your gratitude and follow their example.

Do you consider yourself a giver or a taker? _____

Six Months Review:

_____
_____
_____

Quotation Source Information:

_____
_____
_____

May 15
November 14

> "When a man dies if he can pass enthusiasm
> along to his children, he has left them with
> an estate of incalculable value."

Thomas Edison

We all have passions. What enthusiasms or passions do you share with those with whom you have a relationship?

_____
_____
_____
_____
_____

What would you change in order to ensure that the legacy you leave behind is what you actually want it to be?

_____
_____
_____
_____
_____

Make those changes starting today!!!

Six Months Review:

_____
_____
_____

Quotation Source Information:

_____
_____
_____

May 16
November 15

"The vacuum created by failure to communicate
will quickly be filled with rumor,
misrepresentation, drivel and poison."

C. Northcote Parkinson

Many times we stop communicating with others due to hurt, misunderstanding or other differences. List three people you need to begin communicating with to stop the cycle described in the quote above:

1. _____
   _____

2. _____
   _____

3. _____
   _____

Six Months Review:

_____
_____
_____

Quotation Source Information:

_____
_____
_____

May 17
November 16

"Prosperity is a great teacher, adversity is a greater one."

William Hazlitt

When things are going great we have no reason to grow or learn new skills. It is when times get rough that we call upon what we learned or learn new skills to get us through the situation. List three things you have learned from adversity you have endured in past relationships:

1. _____
   _____

2. _____
   _____

3. _____
   _____

How can you utilize those lessons learned in present and future relationships?

Six Months Review:

_____
_____
_____

Quotation Source Information:

_____
_____
_____

May 18
November 17

Help your brother's boat across,
and your own will reach the shore.

Hindu Proverb

Relationships are many times about giving. List three ways you can reach
your own goals by helping others reach theirs:

1. _____
   _____

2. _____
   _____

3. _____
   _____

Six Months Review:

_____
_____
_____

Quotation Source Information:

_____
_____
_____

May 19
November 18

"Don't talk about yourself;
it will be done when you leave."

Wilson Mizner

People love to talk about themselves. It takes self control to defer that privilege to another. List the things you do that make people want to talk about you in a positive light when you are not present:

_____
_____
_____
_____
_____

Six Months Review:

_____
_____
_____

Quotation Source Information:

_____
_____
_____

May 20
November 19

"There is nothing on this earth
more to be prized than true friendship."

Thomas Aquinas

True friends are rare. List all of the true friends you have had in your lifetime:

_____

_____

_____

_____

_____

What made each friendship so special?

_____

_____

_____

_____

_____

Do you need to do repairs on any of those friendships? Do not hesitate to begin the repair process.

Six Months Review:

_____

_____

_____

Quotation Source Information:

_____

_____

_____

May 21
November 20

"A successful man is one who can lay a firm foundation
with the bricks others have thrown at him."

David Brinkley

We all have critics, no matter how good or bad we are at anything.
Sometimes the criticism is just, sometimes just the ranting of a jealous
or insecure few. List some criticisms you have received that have actually
become positive learning experiences for you:

_____
_____
_____
_____
_____

Six Months Review:

_____
_____
_____

Quotation Source Information:

_____
_____
_____

May 22
November 21

Love and eggs are best when they are fresh.

Russian Proverb

Remember the feelings you get at the start of a new relationship? List ways you can keep love alive in your primary relationships:

_____
_____
_____
_____
_____

Ask those in your primary relationships for their list. Their priorities, needs and wants may differ from yours.

_____
_____
_____

Do these things regularly.

Six Months Review:

_____
_____
_____

Quotation Source Information:

_____
_____
_____

May 23
November 22

Friendship doubles our joy and divides our grief.

Swedish Proverb

Does the quote hold true for all of your friendships? _____

Why or Why not?

_____

_____

_____

List three ways your friendships double your joy:
1. _____

2. _____

3. _____

List three ways your friendships divide your grief:
1. _____

2. _____

3. _____

Six Months Review:

_____

_____

_____

Quotation Source Information:

_____

_____

_____

May 24
November 23

"I have friends in overalls whose friendship I would not swap for the favor of the kings of the world."

Thomas Edison

Make a list of things that you appreciate in all of your friends.

_____
_____
_____
_____
_____

Today contact your friends and share your appreciation.

While you are talking with your friends, ask your friends what they appreciate about you. List below:

_____
_____
_____
_____
_____

Six Months Review:

_____
_____
_____

Quotation Source Information:

_____
_____
_____

May 25
November 24

> "Never part without loving words to
> think of during your absence.
> It may be that you will not meet again in this life."

Jean Paul Richter

Parting may be happy, sad or routine. It may also be anticipation for your next meeting. List five ways you can leave someone with not only loving words, but a loving feeling about you and your relationships:

1. _____
   _____

2. _____
   _____

3. _____
   _____

4. _____
   _____

5. _____
   _____

Six Months Review:
_____
_____
_____

Quotation Source Information:
_____
_____
_____

May 26
November 25

"Never confuse a single defeat with a final defeat."

F. Scott Fitzgerald

In every part of our lives we realize that setbacks are a part of the journey to reach any important goal. It's the same in relationships. When there is commitment to the relationship there is no such thing as defeat, just things we learn to improve the relationship. Some lessons are easily learned, some more difficult.

List three ways you can constructively deal with disappointments in relationships:

1. _____
   _____

2. _____
   _____

3. _____
   _____

Six Months Review:

_____
_____
_____

Quotation Source Information:

_____
_____
_____

May 27
November 26

"Life belongs to the living, and he who lives must be prepared for changes."

Johann Wolfgang von Goethe

The only thing that stays the same in relationships is that they never stay the same. List three ways you can constructively deal with change:

1. _____

   _____

2. _____

   _____

3. _____

   _____

Six Months Review:

_____
_____
_____

Quotation Source Information:

_____
_____
_____

May 28
November 27

"The best gift you can give your children is a good marriage."

Jacqueline L. Kluemper, L.C.S.W.

This has been said many times in many different ways. Children learn about relationships from examples they see in their lives. The kind of relationship their parents have has a profound effect on their lives.

What are your children learning about relationships from you?

_____

_____

_____

What behavior are you modeling for them in the relationship with their other parent?

_____

_____

_____

Would some changes help? If so, list them below:

_____

_____

_____

Six Months Review:

_____

_____

_____

Quotation Source Information:

_____

_____

_____

May 29
November 28

> "When humor goes, there goes civilization."

Erma Bombeck

Is your relationship too serious? Could it use a shot of humor? Think about how you can find humor in your relationships. List them:

_____
_____
_____
_____
_____

Six Months Review:

_____
_____
_____

Quotation Source Information:

_____
_____
_____

May 30
November 29

"The capability for getting along with our neighbor
depends to a large extent on the capacity
for getting along with ourselves."

Eric Hoffer

How do you feel about the way you get along with yourself? In other
words, how do you feel about you?

_____

_____

_____

_____

_____

List your strengths:

_____

_____

_____

_____

_____

Eliminate your weaknesses, strengthen your strengths!!!

Six Months Review:

_____

_____

_____

Quotation Source Information:

_____

_____

_____

May 31
November 30

"Friends are the sunshine of life."

John Hay

We all have had people in our lives who bring a smile to our heart when we think about them. List all of the people who bring sunshine into your life:

_____
_____
_____
_____
_____

Next to each person listed, write how he or she does that.

Go and do the same for others in your life.

Six Months Review:

_____
_____
_____

Quotation Source Information:

_____
_____
_____

June 1
December 1

"The difference between perseverance and obstinacy is that one often comes from a strong will, and the other from a strong won't."

Henry Ward Beecher

Are you being stubborn when flexible would be better? If the issue is important enough to you list some ways you can persevere rather than be obstinate when it comes to your relationships:

_____
_____
_____
_____
_____

Ask those around you for input on this topic.

Six Months Review:

_____
_____
_____

Quotation Source Information:

_____
_____
_____

June 2
December 2

"My life has been filled with terrible misfortune; most of which never happened."

Montaigne

Anticipation of bad things to come in a relationship may be worse than the actual bad events, if they do indeed occur. List ways you can avoid anticipating negative events that most likely will never occur:

_____
_____
_____
_____
_____

Six Months Review:

_____
_____
_____

Quotation Source Information:

_____
_____
_____

June 3
December 3

"I love you!"

We hear it everyday. We say it everyday.
What does it mean to you?

_____
_____
_____

Who do you need to say it more too?

_____
_____
_____

How can you increase the value of this phrase in your life?

_____
_____
_____

Six Months Review:

_____
_____
_____

Quotation Source Information:

_____
_____
_____

June 4
December 4

"Goodness is the only investment that never fails."

Henry David Thoreau

Everyone likes to have good things happen to him or her, even if they refuse to publicly acknowledge it. We even have a tendency to categorize people as good or bad, with not much latitude for the middle ground.

List some people to whom you have not been good enough:

_____
_____
_____
_____
_____

Contact each one today with an act of goodness. Note the experiences above.

Six Months Review:

_____
_____
_____

Quotation Source Information:

_____
_____
_____

June 5
December 5

"The quality of expectations determines the quality of our action."

Andre Godin

Describe your ideal perfect relationship:

_____

_____

In relationships, do your actions meet, exceed or fall short of your expectations? _____

What can you do to increase the level of your action as well as your expectations?

_____

_____

How can you effectively communicate your expectations in relationships?

_____

_____

Do you listen to the expectations that others have for you in relationships?

_____

How can you improve this skill?

_____

_____

Six Months Review:

_____

_____

Quotation Source Information:

_____

_____

June 6
December 6

> "When you choose your friends, don't be short-changed by choosing personality over character."

W. Somerset Maugham

List your five closest friends. Next to person note the character traits that each exhibits. Is the list for each dominated by positive or negative character traits?

1. _____
   _____

2. _____
   _____

3. _____
   _____

4. _____
   _____

5. _____
   _____

How do you feel about the character traits that you exhibit?

_____
_____
_____

Six Months Review:

_____
_____
_____

Quotation Source Information:

_____
_____
_____

June 7
December 7

"No success in public life can compensate for failure in the home."

Benjamin Disraeli

Balancing our personal and professional lives can be a challenge. As our lives progress, priorities change. List ways you can become a greater success at home:

_____

_____

_____

_____

_____

Six Months Review:

_____

_____

_____

Quotation Source Information:

_____

_____

_____

June 8
December 8

"For every minute you remain angry, you give up sixty seconds of peace of mind."

Ralph Waldo Emerson

Anger can be directed in many different directions such as at others, at yourself, at your past, in your present circumstances, etc. Ultimately, this anger can affect your relationships. In which areas are you not experiencing peace of mind?

_____
_____
_____
_____
_____

Seek out ways to make peace in these areas.

Six Months Review:

_____
_____
_____

Quotation Source Information:

_____
_____
_____

June 9
December 9

"An order that can be misunderstood will be misunderstood."

Napoleon Bonaparte

Effective communication is vital to any healthy relationship. How can you improve your communication skills?

_____
_____
_____
_____
_____

Six Months Review:

_____
_____
_____

Quotation Source Information:

_____
_____
_____

June 10
December 10

"Coming together is a beginning.
Keeping together is progress.
Working together is success."

Henry Ford

What does this quote mean to you?

_____

_____

_____

How can it be utilized to improve your most treasured relationships?

_____

_____

_____

Six Months Review:

_____

_____

_____

Quotation Source Information:

_____

_____

_____

June 11
December 11

> "My father gave me the greatest gift anyone could
> give another person, he believed in me."

Jim Valvano

Our self-esteem is rooted in our early home life. However, it is boosted or depleted as we continue through life. List people who have shown that they believe in you:

_____

_____

_____

_____

_____

Contact each today, if possible, and express your appreciation.

List three people that you believe in, note why you believe in them:

1. _____

_____

2. _____

_____

3. _____

_____

Contact each today to make sure that they know you believe in them and why.

Six Months Review:

_____

_____

_____

Quotation Source Information:

_____

_____

_____

June 12
December 12

"An angry man opens his mouth and shuts up his eyes."

Cato

Have you ever been so angry that you spoke (emotionally) without thinking, later regretting your words? List healthy and constructive ways you can express anger:

_____
_____
_____
_____
_____

The next time you get angry, remember to respond utilizing these constructive ways rather than reacting destructively.

Six Months Review:

_____
_____
_____

Quotation Source Information:

_____
_____
_____

June 13
December 13

"The easiest thing to find is fault."

Unknown

Do you pay more attention to strengths or weaknesses in people? Think of three ways to overlook the faults of others you see regularly:

_____
_____
_____
_____
_____

Six Months Review:

_____
_____
_____

June 14
December 14

"It is never too late to become
what you might have been."

George Eliot

What have you always wanted in relationships?

_____
_____
_____
_____
_____

What can you do to become the person who can attain your relationship goals in a win/win scenario?

_____
_____
_____

It is never too late to make those necessary changes. Begin today to achieve those goals.

Six Months Review:

_____
_____
_____

Quotation Source Information:

_____
_____
_____

June 15
December 15

"People are lonely because they build walls
instead of bridges."

Joseph Newton

Loneliness is something we all experience at some time. Taking responsibility for its cause can be an eye opener. Many times rather than reaching out to others, we not only isolate ourselves, but also construct emotional barriers that repel people. List people you have built walls around:

_____

_____

_____

_____

_____

Contact each today and build a bridge. Note the results.

Six Months Review:

_____

_____

_____

Quotation Source Information:

_____

_____

_____

June 16
December 16

"Charity looks at the need, not at the cause."

German Proverb

Part of our duty in life is to help others when they are in need and to ask for help when we are in need. How have others been sensitive to your needs?

_____
_____
_____
_____
_____

How are you are sensitive to the needs of others?

_____
_____
_____
_____
_____

Six Months Review:

_____
_____
_____

Quotation Source Information:

_____
_____
_____

June 17
December 17

"Everyone thinks of changing the world,
but no one thinks of changing himself."

Leo Tolstoy

How honest are you about yourself?

_____

The only person we can change is ourselves. Could you make changes in yourself that would improve your primary relationships?

_____
_____
_____
_____
_____

Six Months Review:

_____
_____
_____

Quotation Source Information:

_____
_____
_____

June 18
December 18

"The last of the human freedoms is to choose one's attitudes."

Victor Frank

You, not those around you, are responsible for your attitude. Think about ways to maintain control of your attitude, even in rough times:

_____
_____
_____
_____
_____

Six Months Review:

_____
_____
_____

Quotation Source Information:

_____
_____
_____

June 19
December 19

"Most people walk in and out of your life,
but only friends leave footprints in your heart."

Unknown

Record the people who have left lifelong footprints in your life:

1. _____
   _____

2. _____
   _____

3. _____
   _____

Note the significance of each footprint.
Contact each person today to express your gratitude.

Six Months Review:

_____
_____
_____

June 20
December 20

"To see what is right and not to do it, is want of courage."

Confucius Analects

There are times when we know what the right thing to do is, yet lack the courage to do the right thing. Think about times when you have chosen not to do the right thing at the right time. What was the result?

_____
_____
_____
_____
_____

What could you have done differently?

_____
_____
_____
_____
_____

Six Months Review:

_____
_____
_____

Quotation Source Information:

_____
_____
_____

June 21
December 21

"The day you have your first real laugh at yourself
is the day you really grow up."

Marilyn S. Possett, L.C.S.W.

When was the day you really had your first laugh at yourself?

_____

List all the details (circumstances, people involved, etc.):

_____
_____
_____
_____
_____

How did it improve relationships with yourself and others?

_____
_____
_____
_____
_____

Six Months Review:

_____
_____
_____

Quotation Source Information:

_____
_____
_____

June 22
December 22

"The bend in the road is not the end of the road unless you refuse to take the turn."

Unknown

Register some key turning points in relationships you have experienced. How did they affect the relationships?

_____
_____
_____
_____
_____

Did you make the right choice? _____

Note above what you learned from each experience.

Six Months Review:

_____
_____
_____

June 23
December 23

"If you were arrested for kindness,
would there be enough evidence to convict you?"

Unknown

List all the ways you can think of to express kindness to others:

_____
_____
_____
_____
_____

Note the responses you receive from other as you express kindness to everyone you come in contact with.

_____
_____
_____
_____
_____

Six Months Review:

_____
_____
_____

June 24
December 24

"Wear a smile and have friends,
wear a frown and have wrinkles."

George Eliot

How does your attitude affect your friendships?

_____
_____
_____
_____
_____

Meet with three of your most trusted friends and ask them to critique your attitude. Be open-minded when listening to their impressions. Record the results here:

_____
_____
_____
_____
_____

Six Months Review:

_____
_____
_____

Quotation Source Information:

_____
_____
_____

June 25
December 25

"Appreciation can make a day, even change a life."

Margaret Cousins

One of the most often heard complaints about a relationship is some-one is not feeling appreciated. Everyone wants to be valued. Record ways people have shown appreciation to you:

_____
_____
_____
_____
_____

How good are you at showing appreciation to others?

_____
_____
_____
_____

Six Months Review:

_____
_____

Quotation Source Information:

_____
_____
_____

June 26
December 26

"Am I not destroying my enemies when I make friends of them?"

Abraham Lincoln

Whom do you consider your enemies. Why? Is it still valid?

1. _____
   _____

2. _____
   _____

3. _____
   _____

4. _____
   _____

5. _____
   _____

If appropriate, contact each today to mend the relationship. Note your progress and results.

Six Months Review:

_____
_____
_____

Quotation Source Information:

_____
_____
_____

June 27
December 27

"Time is what we want most, but what we use worst."

William Penn

In relationships we waste time for several reasons, the most common is taking others for granted. Over time we have a tendency to lose that sense of urgency and priority as other people or circumstances may introduce themselves. List ways you can make better use of time in your primary relationships:

_____

_____

_____

_____

_____

Six Months Review:

_____

_____

_____

Quotation Source Information:

_____

_____

_____

June 28
December 28

"True love does not come by finding the perfect
person, but by learning to see
an imperfect person perfectly."

Jason Jordan

One of the great equalizers in relationships is that it is the joining of two or more imperfect people. While the agendas differ greatly between personal and professional relationships, creating win/win scenarios may involve overlooking irrelevant imperfections in others, just as they overlook certain imperfections in you. How can you overcome the imperfections in others?

_____
_____
_____

How can others overcome your imperfections?

_____
_____
_____

Six Months Review:

_____
_____
_____

Quotation Source Information:

_____
_____
_____

June 29
December 29

"Teamwork is the fuel that allows common people to attain uncommon results."

Unknown

All relationships involve teamwork. It does not matter if the *team* is your family, primary personal relationship, co-workers, friends, etc., you are a part of a team. Understanding that will help you to *play well with others*. List ways to develop teamwork in your everyday relationships:

_____
_____
_____
_____
_____

Today, discuss these ideas with your primary relationships. Write the results in the space below:

_____
_____
_____
_____
_____

Six Months Review:

_____
_____
_____

June 30
December 30

"To laugh often and much; to win the respect of intelligent people and the affection of children…to leave the world a better place…to know even one life has breathed easier because you have lived. This is to have succeeded."

Ralph Waldo Emerson

Read the above quote carefully. How can you work toward living the way Emerson describes to reach his definition of success?

_____
_____
_____
_____
_____

Six Months Review:
_____
_____
_____

Quotation Source Information:
_____
_____
_____

July 1
December 31

"God grant me the serenity to accept the people
I cannot change, the courage to change the one I can,
and the wisdom to know it's me."

Unknown

(A variation of an excerpt from
"The Serenity Prayer" by Reinhold Neibuhr)

List the one most important thing you want to change about you.

_____
_____
_____

Do it!!!!!!

Six Months Review:

_____
_____
_____

Congratulations!

You have completed a milestone and made a major investment in yourself both personally and professionally. If you are in the first six months of this book you have already learned much about yourself and the qualities that are needed to have powerful relationships. If you just completed the last six months of this book you have completed a year-long excursion that has polished the skills needed to further your journey down the road to powerful relationships. Re-read the information in the beginning of this book, it will offer more insight into your relationships than it ever has.

Now that you have new knowledge, share it with others. By helping others to become more powerful, you make yourself more powerful.

Relationships involve giving! By completing this volume, you have more to share than you ever have in your fascinating life.

Again, congratulations!

Peter Biadasz and Marilyn S. Possett, L.C.S.W.

Conclusion

You have just finished the footwork, so now is the time to put it to real work. That is, make it work for you in your relationships, both personal and professional. You have absorbed the quotations and learned about the author or the quote source. In the first six months, you have fully completed each daily lesson. In the second six months, you have carefully reviewed the assignments and made the appropriate adjustments. During this period of time, you have practiced what you have learned. All of these completed tasks have made you a more powerful person. You did it on your own. You did it in private. Now, fully infuse that power into your daily private and public life. Release the power of effective relationships into all of your personal and professional life activities.

You already know that powerful people have powerful relationships. You read about them in books, magazines and newspapers. You see them around you. You have learned from them in the past. So, if you have carefully read this book and diligently completed the exercises, then you have made the choice to be powerful. And, quality and powerful relationships nurture successful and powerful living. Now, go forth, knowing you have the power to be successful in any area you choose, for powerful people have powerful relationships.

About the Authors

Peter Biadasz (pronounced *bee-ahd-ish*) has been working with groups since 1989 in various capacities including president, consultant, speaker as well as a very active member. A graduate of Florida State University with a major in Psychology and a minor in Counseling, Peter's passion for and expertise in the areas of the networking of people has aided many in receiving and giving more in both their personal and professional relationships. Peter teaches that networking is all about relationships, whether it be at home or in the office. Business groups that Peter works with experience an increase in the quality and quantity of leads passed, an increase in the quantity and quality of group members and an overall excitement for networking as never experienced before as group members transform into quality maturing networkers. Peter has been known to utilize his trumpet to liven up speaking engagements.

The father of an incredible son and precious daughter, Peter is also the author of *More Leads: The Complete Handbook For Tips Groups, Leads Groups and Networking Groups* and co-author of the *Power Series*. Over the years Peter has also written several articles on various aspects of interpersonal relationships. Feel free to visit Peter at *www.getmore-leads.net* and *www.bepowerful.net*.

Marilyn Possett is a Licensed Psychotherapist practicing at Laureate Psychiatric Clinic and Hospital in Tulsa, Oklahoma. Her focus is in Cognitive-Behavioral Therapy and she has had specific training in marriage and family therapy, as well as extensive experience helping people with their relationships.

Born and raised in Grand Rapids, Michigan, Marilyn moved with her husband and children to Los Angeles, California, and then to the Midwest where they have lived for eighteen years. Marilyn has been married to her husband, Richard, for over forty-one years. In addition to her three children (Nicole, Richard and Michael) and son-in-law, Daryl, she has three grandchildren, Braden, Rebekah and Hailey. Her hobbies are digital photography, walking, training and playing with her two Golden Retrievers and, of course, her grandchildren.

While raising her children and moving around the country with her family, Marilyn attended various colleges. She earned a Bachelor of Science degree in Family Relations and Child Development from Oklahoma State University and a Master's Degree in Clinical Social Work from the University of Oklahoma. She is licensed to practice individual, group and marital therapy. Marilyn has given presentations and written articles on interpersonal skills, stress management, depression and anxiety; and she has co-authored a training manual on Cognitive-Behavioral Therapy. You can visit with Marilyn at *mpossett@sbcglobal.net*.

For more information, or to send us your favorite quotes and assignments, please visit *www.bepowerful.net*.

Index of Individuals Quoted

Index of Topics Quoted

Note: Many quotes may fit into more than one category.

A Chuncated Approach

'Power~Series'

Ben Franklin was a brilliant gentleman and a great moral exemplar. Furthermore, he possessed a myriad of supremely admirable skills and talents. One of Franklin's many gifts was the extraordinary ability to see potential and then realize it. An area in which this aptitude was truly manifested was in the development of Franklin's moral excellence. Early on in life he had actualized his very own *chuncated* training regimen for goodness called the thirteen virtues. Franklin wrote out a list of these ideals and had them printed in a table made up of seven columns (one for each day of the week) and thirteen rows (one for each virtue). He then placed a black spot in the appropriate square each time he failed to live that day in agreement with a particular attribute. At first, Franklin concentrated on only one quality each week, hoping to keep its row clear of spots while paying no special attention to the other characteristics. Over thirteen weeks, he worked through the whole matrix. Then he repeated the process, finding that with repetition the table got less and less spotty. Franklin wrote in his autobiography that, though he fell short of perfection: "I was, by the endeavor, a better and happier man than I otherwise should have been if I had not attempted it." From this approach, Franklin *chuncated* himself to moral excellence one day at a time. For a full explanation of the virtues, please go to www.school-for-champions.com or simply Google the internet.

As you can see, *chuncated* learning has been around at least, if not longer, since the beginning of the republic. It is a time-tested methodology of erudition. It is a highly effective way of developing character and personality, acquiring information, and applying knowledge. We call this technique the Chuncated Learning System, or "CLS." CLS is a compelling way of cultivating positive growth and change in both your personal and professional lives. For this reason, chuncated learning is the chosen method that is used in the 'Power~Series' books. CLS is a highly cogent manner for changing personality style gradually by mastering and applying facts and ideas incrementally.

A big part of CLS is the small. This is because the process takes a large body of work and breaks it down into little enjoyable pieces. CLS is effective because it teaches a big concept in small daily bite sizes of knowledge. It is a wise-way we term "chunking." The approach takes a huge hunk of education and breaks it down into wee nuggets for easier learning. It is very much like baby steps. That is, scholarship in tiny short strides.

In each 'Power~Series' book, there are exercises to be completed, reviewed, and revised over a period of one year. These tasks are assigned as home school, to be done daily in a fun, fast, and easy fashion. Empirically, we have come to know that the earthborn learn best from consistent daily study and practice. This mode easily reframes and reinforces the specific subject matter. So then, over many days and weeks, new knowledge is accumulated and a new awareness of oneself emerges, shaping a powerfully enhanced neo-personality style.

With each simple assignment thoroughly and thoughtfully completed, the student of a 'Power~Series' book receives a modicum of wisdom in the form of a small reward, a little flash of accomplishment. It is an ecstatic titillation of self-admiration; a euphoric sense of self-confidence emboldened by achievement. This sensation is the wonderfully good feeling of a personal job well done. And each shot of "feel-good" is like a hulking reward reinforcing a newly learned chunked concept. By gradually shaping, hunk-by-chunk, your thoughts and actions, CLS strongly influences an improved personality style having the power of presence and poise. It hones your latent power-driven traits and talents for a new and improved powerfully you.

Furthermore, CLS was adopted for the 'Power~Series' books because of its simple and straightforward approach to learning. In the hurly-burly of modern society, it is often difficult, as an adult, to continue one's education and self development. The strictures of home, work, and family responsibilities can frequently retard your personal growth and the capability to improve the self. CLS, with its "chunking" process, helps to materially mitigate the constraints of time. By simply setting aside a very small part of your busy day and focusing on learning in bite sizes, you can grow more powerful with your newly applied knowledge, one day at a time.

A  Book

The 'Power Series' Books

The 'Power Series' books mean what they say and say what they mean. They are powerful and contain the dynamism to make you a power-driven person. The books are about readers learning how to effectively acquire and utilize productive power in all facets of their lives. The books are not concerned with dominion, authority, and control. These books are about health, wealth and happiness. The 'Power Series' books provide the principles and practices that can produce a full and highly successful lifestyle.

There are many elements that make a power person. Such essential elements as relationships, leadership, networking, teaching, listening, learning, spirituality, character, and health make for a powerful life. The material and information in the 'Power Series' books speaks to the subject of what it takes to be powerful in living life. The aforementioned areas are just a summary of what it takes to be a powerful person. The syllabus can go on ad infinitum. Currently, 'Power Series' book titles include:

Powerful People Have Powerful Character
Powerful People Overcome Powerful Failures
Powerful People Play Powerful Golf
Powerful People Have Powerful Health
Powerful People Are Powerful I.T. Professionals
Powerful People Are Powerful Learners
Powerful People Are Powerful Listeners
Powerful People Are Powerful Leaders
Powerful People Have Powerful Money
Powerful People Are Powerful Networkers
Powerful People Are Powerful Performers

Powerful People Have Powerful Personalities
Powerful People Are Powerful Risk Managers
Powerful People Are Powerful Teachers

More Titles to Be Released Next Year

To learn more about the 'Power Series' as well as to order additional books, please visit *www.bepowerful.net*. The 'Power Series' books are the production of Peter Biadasz and Richard Possett.

978-0-595-41138-2
0-595-41138-X